Evolution, Morality,
and the Meaning of Life

PHILOSOPHY AND SOCIETY

General Editor: Marshall Cohen

Also in this series:

Evolution, Morality, and the Meaning of Life

JEFFRIE G. MURPHY

ROWMAN AND LITTLEFIELD
Totowa, New Jersey

First published in the United States 1982 by
Rowman and Littlefield, 81 Adams Drive, Totowa, New Jersey 07512.

Library of Congress Cataloging in Publication Data

Murphy, Jeffrie G.
    Evolution, morality, and the meaning of life.

    (Philosophy and society)
    Based on a series of lectures delivered at the
University of Virginia in October 1981.
    Includes index.
    1. Ethics—Addresses, essays, lectures.
    2. Evolution—Addresses, essays, lectures.
    3. Sociobiology—Addresses, essays, lectures.
    4. Meaning (Philosophy)—Addresses, essays, lectures.
    I. Title. II. Series.
    BJ1012.M88   1982   171   82-9782
    ISBN 0-8476-7147-X   AACR2

Printed in the United States of America

To the memory of
Helen Canacakos
1905–1981
and to
Gertrude Canacakos

Contents

Preface

This book is based upon a series of lectures I delivered at the University of Virginia in October of 1981 at the kind invitation of the Committee on Comparative Study of Individual and Society and under the sponsorship of the Center for Advanced Studies.

The lectures were aimed at a general audience, and thus great effort was made to eliminate technicality, boring and cumbersome references, and the inane in-group excursions increasingly characteristic of my own discipline of philosophy. The present book, though involving a considerable expansion of the lectures, is offered in the same spirit. My friend Tony Woozley, a distinguished member of the University of Virginia faculty, has always maintained that anything worth saying in philosophy can be said in plain English. I have attempted at all times here to follow his maxim. It is my hope, of course, that I have not erred in the opposite direction and produced a work of terrible superficiality. If I have, the fact that I have already cashed my honorarium check will no doubt assist me in bearing the shame with dignity and tranquility.

Tempe, Arizona
March, 1982

Acknowledgments

I am very grateful to the Committee on Comparative Study of Individual and Society and the Center for Advanced Studies, University of Virginia, for the invitation to deliver the lectures upon which this book is based. In order to deliver lectures that would, in my judgment, be in the spirit of the Committee's purpose, I was forced to think about a variety of issues I might otherwise have left unexplored. I, at least, have benefited from this diversion from my normal course of research, and thus I hope that I have, at least in part, fulfilled the purposes of this fine interdisciplinary committee.

I have visited the University of Virginia several times in recent years, and each time I have come away grateful for the hospitality I have received and for the intellectual benefit derived from interaction with the fine minds at this institution. On this occasion, I would like to single out the following persons for particular thanks: R. S. Khare (my very kind host), Cora Diamond, Robert Kretsinger, David Little, and Tony Woozley.

Though most of this book involves new departures for me, the opening chapter grows out of two previous efforts of mine: a public lecture in February 1981 at the University of Arizona in its lecture series "Religion and Human Values" and my essay "Hume and Kant on the Social Contract" (in my *Retribution, Justice and Therapy: Essays in the Philosophy of Law*, Dordrecht and Boston: D. Reidel, 1979). (In my essay on Kant and Hume, I closed with the conviction that Hume's analysis of morality, though in many ways brilliant, is ultimately defeated by a rationalistic analysis that is

Kantian in character. As will be obvious to anyone who heard the lectures or reads this book, my confidence in this conviction has, to put it mildly, been considerably shaken.) Many persons provided helpful comments on the lecture and the essay, and I am extremely grateful to them all. I want to single out Professors Merrilee and Wesley Salmon for special thanks in this regard.

Michael Ruse and Merrilee Salmon generously read and commented on the entire manuscript of the Virginia lectures, and I am very grateful for their help and encouragement. Also, for more limited but still very generous and valuable help, let me also thank Jane Maienschein, John Alcock, and Roy Spece.

Finally, I want to thank my wife, Ellen Canacakos. My work is always improved through her thoughtful discussion and criticism; and my life is always improved by her enormous capacity to put everything in its proper perspective.

The book is dedicated to the memory of Helen Canacakos and to Gertrude Canacakos. I have received warmth and kindness from these two wonderful women and have seen them exemplify a kind of natural morality that has nothing to do with a reluctant answer to the stern call of duty, but instead comes from the heart. They have helped me to realize how terribly silly are those philosophical theories that would exclude such spontaneity of decent feeling from the moral realm.

Introduction

I am sorry to say that I have no 'consolatory view' as to [the] dignity of man: I am content that man will probably advance, and care not very much whether we are looked at as mere savages in a remotely distant future. Many thanks for your last note—
Yours affectionately, C. Darwin
    I have noted in a Manchester newspaper a rather good squib, showing that I have proved 'might is right,' and therefore that Napolean is right and every cheating tradesman is also right—

CHARLES DARWIN *(To Lyell, May 4, 1860)*

A philosopher, being escorted to deliver a lecture on "The Universe," was asked by his host why he had not chosen to lecture on something else. He replied, "There isn't anything else." I feel in a somewhat similar position as I am about to launch a book under the rather pretentious title "Evolution, Morality, and the Meaning of Life." The title seems so hopelessly vague and general that it will no doubt seem almost certain to invite terrible superficiality, if not total vacuousness. Thus, in order to attempt to quell such fears at the outset, I want to begin by explaining briefly what I have in mind to explore in the present volume. My intent is to persuade you that my topic, though indeed general, is not hopelessly so.

My original interest in the topic of the book developed as I attempted to familiarize myself with the intellectual and scientific movement generally labeled "sociobiology." Though temperamentally suspicious of anything that seems trendy, I felt that, as a legal and moral philospher, I should at least have a look at the literature that was claimed to have great significance for morality and moral philosophy. I knew that sociobiology involved an attempt to apply evolutionary thinking to morality; and I also knew that, at least in general terms, such attempts were not new. Hume, Nietzsche, and (of course) Darwin himself had all developed theoretical accounts of the origin of morality and had all stressed that these accounts were, in some general sense, evolutionary—though only Darwin, of course, applied the specific mechanism of natural selection in his account. For all of their differences in detail, these three thinkers shared the belief that a proper understanding of the causal origins of morality would undermine a certain rationalistic pretentiousness about morality that had been encouraged by certain schools of philosophy and theology. They in a sense reduced (or even "demoted") morality by seeing it as something "human—all too human" (or even "animal—all too animal") instead of something spiritual or divine in nature. (Perhaps we should call these theories "anti-inflationary" instead of "reductionist.") Severed from cosmic authority, morality would henceforth have to be seen as, at best, relatively guaranteed by the empirical circumstances of human nature or, at worst, as not guaranteed at all, as arbitrary. Sociobiology should be seen as a continuation of this pattern of thought.

Even when the actual intentions of these thinkers were benign (as was certainly the case with the morally conservative Hume and Darwin), the actual impact of their ideas was often seen as devastating. The threatened tradition conceived of morality as founded on the special and unique dignity of man—a precious "something" that distinguished him from the brutes. In traditional religious formulations (e.g., in Christianity) this something was conceived as an immortal soul—a kind of precious jewel possessed only by members of the human species. In secular theories within the same tradition (e.g., that of Immanuel Kant), the special something was regarded as an attribute or capacity possessed by human beings and by no other creatures: the attribute of autonomous rationality. Without such attributes, it was thought, morality as we know it would disappear. For there would be no reason for continuing to embrace those special moral requirements that were thought to attach uniquely to human beings (e.g., the *right* not to be killed and eaten, experimented on without consent, etc.). We would be in the position of being forced in consistency to regard much worse treatment of human beings than is now allowed to be morally permissible or to regard much better treatment of animals as henceforth obligatory in some strong sense.

Not only was morality (and its crucial foundation in the essential dignity of man) to be undercut, but also threatened was the idea that human life in any sense has meaning, significance, or purpose. This is a related threat, of course, because, as Robert Nozick has argued, we tend to take people very seriously from the moral point of view because we regard them as creatures capable of leading meaningful lives. But the threat also transcends moral concerns because most of us want to live lives that *matter*—not just morally matter, but matter in all kinds of ways: aesthetic, prudential, political, romantic, erotic, athletic, etc. But what if *nothing* matters? This depressing question seems at least raised by those theories that, replacing a teleological outlook on man and his place in nature with a purely mechanistic one, seem to deprive us of the comfort that may come in viewing the universe as a special home for the human species. Deprived of transcendent meaning, we may be forced to acknowledge that our lives matter only in some limited and parochial way—the same way the lives of other animals may matter. But, for many persons, this is equivalent to thinking that their lives do not matter at all and are absurd. (Note how frequently, and quite unfairly in my judgment, the metaphors whereby one expresses the sense that human life is absurd involve comparison of a human life to that of an animal: "He leads a dog's life," "Look at us, going about these routine tasks like so many ants climbing up a hill," etc. Comparisons with insect life are regarded as particularly odious, which may explain why Edward O. Wilson's work in sociobiology, grounded in his research in entomology, occasions so much emotional hysteria in his critics.)

As you can see, my attempt to understand and assess sociobiology has led me into diverse collatoral explorations, many of them quite new for me. In this book, I intend to share these explorations with you, not as an expert (who could be an expert on these matters?), but as one intelligent and generally educated student to other intelligent and generally educated students. For this volume, I shall divide my concerns as follows:

Chapter 1: Morality, Religion, and the Meaning of Life. In this chapter I shall do very little that is original. Rather I shall draw upon and synthesize the work of others (especially Hume and Nietzsche) in order to set a general background for the issue of evolution, morality, and the meaning of life. Specifically I shall explore this question: What exactly is it to believe that one's life and one's actions have a significant meaning or purpose, and why might one take comfort in a cosmic or transcendent foundation for such a belief and feel threatened by an account that seems to undermine such a foundation? I shall suggest that the comfort provided by transcendent foundations is illusory and that the fear that morality and meaning are more fragile on a reductionist account than on other more cosmic accounts is unjustified. The foundations of morality are in fact rationally fragile on *all* accounts, naturalistic or supernaturalistic, and thus a certain rationalistic pretentiousness about morality is undermined. It is a virtue of evolutionary accounts of morality to stress this, and I close the first chapter by expressing sympathy with such accounts. I am convinced that important insights on the nature of morality are to be gained by theories that are, in some general sense, evolutionary in nature.

Chapter 2: Scientific Creationism and the Darwinian Revolution. It is not enough, of course, simply to speak in very general terms of the evolutionary origins of morality. One needs a specific and detailed account in order to raise mere chat to the level of theory; and where better to begin this than with Darwin himself? Thus, in the original lecture series, I began at this point exploring Darwin's own account of the origins of morality. In commenting on the manuscript, however, Michael Ruse suggested that the transition was too abrupt—that a discussion of Darwin's general theory was needed to pave the way for the material specifically relevant to ethics. Reflection persuaded me that he was correct, and so the present chapter—not a part of the original lecture series—has been added here. This book is, after all, aimed at an audience of nonspecialists, and so it is unreasonable to presuppose a close familiarity with Darwin's general theory on the part of the reader. (Even many biology students, I have discovered, are surprisingly ignorant of Darwin's own views.) Darwin's views on morality are best understood in the context of the revolution he effected, not just in biology, but in our whole understanding of man and his place in the universe. Of course there is even now an active and vocal counterrevolution—a group of fundamentalist zealots exploiting and misrepresenting disagreements among evolutionary biologists in order to push, under the banner of "scientific creationism," their own brand of pseudo-science. Darwin had opponents of nearly identical views in his own day—only then they called themselves practicioners of "natural religion" or "natural theology." To understand the present conflicts between evolutionists and scientific creationists, it is useful to explore the nineteenth century conflict between Darwinians and their natural theology opponents. This too will be done in the current chapter. Chapter One suggested that rational theology fails in its quest to provide an objective foundation for morality. In this chapter I shall suggest that the moral failure is simply a part of a bigger failure—namely, a failure to provide an adequate understanding of the world and our place in it. This is not a general attack on religion (some of my best friends are religious), but only on religion conceived as the objective and rationally provable foundation for evaluation and understanding. The best in religion is ill-served when trotted out as pseudo-science, a point David Hume put very nicely in this way: "In proportion to my veneration for true religion, is my abhorrence of vulgar superstition."

Chapter 3: Darwin and the Origin of Morality. Having explored the nature and importance of Darwin's general theory, I shall in this chapter examine in detail and critically evaluate his account (primarily in *The Descent of Man*) of morality and the moral sense (conscience).

Chapter 4: Sociobiology, Altruism, and the Reduction of Morality. In the final chapter I shall explore the contemporary literature of sociobiology, particularly the work of Edward O. Wilson. My final evaluation of sociobiology will be mixed. I believe that it has some very serious deficiencies, but I also believe that it has more profound implications for moral philosophy than many of its humanist detractors are prepared to admit. Its claims to give us an ethic for the future are overblown, but its ability to undermine moral philosophy as traditionally practiced is considerable. At the very least sociobiology gives us additional reason for believing that such philosophers as Hume and Nietzsche were on to something when they claimed that the rational foundations for morality are fragile indeed. The *Conclusion* contains a few general closing remarks about morality and the meaning of life and will bring my part of the book to an end.

Following what I have written, I have added as Appendix A the complete text of Judge William R. Overton's opinion in the 1982 case *McLean v. The Arkansas Board of Education*. In that case the court had to rule on the constitutionality of an Arkansas statute requiring that "scientific creationism" be given equal time along with Darwinian evolutionary theory in science classes in Arkansas public schools. The statute was challenged by persons claiming that it violated the First Amendment to the Constitution in two ways: (1) it represented the kind of establishment of religion prohibited by the First Amendment and (2) it violated the right to academic freedom derivable from the free speech clause of the First Amendment. It is important to remember (but often forgotten in the heat of political debate) that we do not live in a pure democracy. We live in a *constitutionally limited* democracy. The amendments that constitute the Bill of Rights in the Constitution in effect say this: There are some rights so basic and fundamental that they may not be violated simply because a democratic majority happens to desire to do so. Rights of this fundamental nature (e.g., freedom of speech) may be encumbered by the state only if it has a compelling reason (e.g., national security) for so doing. Enacting into law some group's religious preferences certainly cannot be a compelling reason; indeed, given the establishment of religion clause, it is not even a permissible reason. These issues are explored in detail in Judge Overton's opinion, and it should serve to put the abstract philosophical discussion contained in this book into an immediate context of practical importance. Though in most respects I welcome and admire Judge Overton's opinion (certainly its conclusion), it does exude a level of confidence about science that my Humean tendencies toward skepticism are reluctant to let pass utterly without challenge. For this reason I was very happy to come across Larry Laudan's note "Science at the Bar: Causes for Concern" (published here as Appendix B). Laudan, a Professor of History and Philosophy of Science at the University of Pittsburgh, attacks the conception of science that Judge Overton (under the influence, no doubt, of expert witnesses) adopted in the Arkansas case. Though Laudan himself welcomes the verdict, he has serious doubts about the justification offered by Overton for that verdict—particularly Overton's attempts to characterize the essential nature of science in order to distinguish it from religion. Neither Overton's opinion nor Laudan's note represent the last word on these complex matters, of course, but the controversy between them should provide an excellent starting point for discussion of the issues and thus should both expand and complement the contents of the present book. As I close my book with a discussion of a legal case, I realize that my vocation as a philosopher of law comes to haunt me even when I set out to work in what I think will be a new and unrelated area of research.

1

Morality, Religion, and the Meaning of Life

Callow Youth:	"Mr. Coward, is life really worth living?"
Noel Coward:	"But, my dear boy, what *else* would we do with it?"

It is, I think, instructive to view basic human institutions and activities in terms of the fundamental human desires—perhaps even needs—to which those institutions and activities are responsive.[1] One such desire or need is to feel *at home* in the world—i.e., to feel that one's presence in the world is appropriate or fitting because the world is a place where one *belongs,* a place where one is not (or at least not totally) an alien stranger. (This is no doubt at least part of what Freud had in mind when he suggested that human beings project infantile desires onto the universe.)

A sense of belonging is aided, and may even depend upon, the belief that one can *understand* the world in which one lives and can *understand* one's place in it, that the framework in which one lives is an *intelligible* one. One wants to feel that one is more like a character in a good, solid Victorian novel than like a character in a novel by Kafka or a play by Pinter or Beckett.

There are at least two different, though related, ways in which one can seek to understand or find the world intelligible: by asking *how* and by asking *why.* In the first case, one seeks to discover how the world *works*—what explains the complex and interrelated occurrences of which we form a part. In the second case, one

9

inquires into the *purposes* or *ends* of things. The first inquiry is mainly factual: what can I *know?* The second inquiry is mainly evaluative or moral: how *should* I live? And these questions are of course related because it would seem quite irrational, even crazy, to value things on the basis of wildly false beliefs about the workings of the world.

Religion, in my view, generally has been responsive to *both* of the basic human desires outlined above. Most of its variations—at least most of those that form a central part of the heritage of western civilization—have contained or presupposed accounts of both the how and the why of things (e.g., the Genesis creation myth is clearly a theory of *how;* the myth of the fall is clearly a moral theory of *why.*)

In its "how" capacity, religion competes with (and has perhaps been superseded by) a rather more sophisticated institution or activity that is also responsive to the desire for explanation, namely, empirical science.[2] This is an issue to be explored in Chapter 2. My primary concern in the present chapter, however, is with religion in its "why" capacity—in its presentation of moral ends and purposes. These purposes are to give us not just a set of obligations (which, as we all know, can be tedious burdens), but also a comforting sense that human life in general (and thus our own life) has *meaning* or *significance.* Or, to put the point negatively, religion seeks to erase any sense that our lives are ridiculous, pointless, or absurd. Here religion seems to compete with (and could perhaps be superseded by) secular moral philosophy; and it is to this competition that I shall now turn.

As a start toward coming to grips with this issue, let us consider what it might mean to claim—with some significance—that human life in general (and thus one's own life) is absurd. In moments of despair such a claim might represent little more than a person's expression of unhappiness or personal loneliness (e.g., over ill health, loss of a job, or abandonment by a loved one). Such expressions are sad and touching, of course, because the situations to which they are responses are ones with which we, as caring human beings, can empathize. But they lack what might be called metaphysical or philosophical significance in that they purport to make no *general* claim about the human condition, about people and their place in the universe, but are rather responses to what is seen as a *departure* from what is expected or at least thought possible—i.e., a way of living that clearly does matter and is really not absurd (the having of good health, a satisfying job, the presence of loved ones, etc.). Thus these expressions are a problem more for the psychiatrist than for the philosopher or theologian. The sense in which philosophers and theologians seek to respond to the claim that human life is perhaps absurd is where this claim is meant to convey a quite general or universal truth about the human condition—namely, that ultimately *no* human life really matters, that every human life (and thus one's own) is in some sense absurd or lacking in real meaning or significance *regardless* of how much one may enjoy its satisfactions. For, according to the metaphysical claim of absurdity, there is an important sense in which even *these* do not matter.

What could one possibly mean by a claim so general and so ambitious in scope? The philosopher Thomas Nagel has suggested that we might get some guidance on this issue from considering what we mean by the word "absurd" in ordinary human life and discourse. According to Nagel, we tend to describe as absurd (perhaps even as comically absurd) any situation where there is a striking conflict or tension between the pretentiousness or solemnity surrounding the situation, on the one hand, and the actual reality of the situation on the other. As examples, we might consider such things as the following: I am about to deliver my Nobel Prize acceptance speech and my pants fall down revealing the word "Monday" embroidered on my bikini underpants; a local citizen is given the "Humanitarian of the Year" award and is revealed the next day to be involved in such underworld activities as fraud, drug dealing, and murder; or the remark once quoted by Dylan Thomas: "How can that man have written such great devotional poetry? Why last week I saw him fall downstairs in his suspenders!"

Now could there be anything about human life *in general* that manifests this tension or conflict between pretension and reality? According to Nagel, there is: the seriousness with which we take and pursue our lives (this is the pretension) in conflict with the perpetual possibility of regarding everything about which we are serious as open to doubt (this is the reality). To put the point another way: the things in life that matter to us the most are the

very things we find ourselves unable to justify by rationally compelling arguments. What we find most important is for us *ultimate*
in importance—i.e., the very thing that provides the values in
terms of which everything else is justified. But can these ultimate
values themselves be justified? *No*, and indeed this is part of what
it means to say that they are ultimate. But if they cannot be
justified, are they perhaps then arbitrary, and thus all things based
on them arbitrary, and thus *everything* ultimately arbitrary? If so,
this does indeed make human life absurd in a very strong sense.

Let me give an example to illustrate the point at issue here. What
Nagel calls the seriousness of life is not a kind of pompous
solemnity; rather it is simply the fact that we use *energy* to pursue
our lives. We throw ourselves into the future with projects and
plans and act as though these are worthwhile. But are they?
Consider something as simple as the following pattern of reasoning:

"I am going to school."

"Why?"

"In order, among other things, to make a good income in life."

"Why?"

"Well, in order to buy some important items for my life—for
example, adequate health care."

"But why is health care important?"

"Because it makes us healthy."

"But why is health important?"

"Because it makes us happy."

"But why is it important to be happy?"

"Shut up! It just *is*, damn it! Can't you see that?"

The moral here is this: At some point in a chain of justification
one simply digs in one's heels and *stops* with something (happiness
perhaps) that is just *accepted* as a value, not proven to be one. But if
this is so, what guarantee do we have that this value—since it must
be accepted rather than proven or rationally justified—is not
simply arbitrary and thus all values based on it (i.e., the moral
fabric of our *entire lives*) arbitrary? The "whys", it seems, logically
outlast all possible answers—a comprehensive skepticism that one
might well find terribly disquieting.[3]

Religion can, in at least one of its capacities, be seen as attempting to address itself to this fear of arbitrariness and subjectivism

and its resulting sense that human life is, after all, a pretty futile and silly business. For religion attempts to hold out a promise that at least certain values *can* be defended as ultimate, perhaps through seeing them as, in some sense, commanded by the will of God. On this view, God is the objective judge who saves our values from being arbitrary and the lives we lead based on those values from being absurd. Religion can in this way be seen as addressed to the deep worry expressed by Ivan in Dostoevsky's *Brothers Karamazov*—the worry that "without God all things are permitted." For if all things are permitted and are equally valuable, then the very concept of value begins to lose significance.

Does the religious response work? As a matter of *fact*, it may work psychologically for some people—i.e., it may give them a kind of comfort and sense of security about these matters, a *belief* that life is meaningful and thus not absurd. But the comfort provided by a belief is a very different issue from the truth or reasonableness of that belief—i.e., the comfort could be a matter of illusion or self-deception. Thus the question I want to explore is this: Can the belief in God provide a *reasonable* basis for claiming that absurdity in life is avoided and that meaningfulness is thereby guaranteed? I am quite skeptical that it can.

There are, of course, some rather silly, even if rather common, versions of the religious attempt to guarantee significance to human life. As an example consider the claim that was common in the Middle Ages and responsible for the religious persecution of many astronomers that the earth is the center of the universe. Religious orthodoxy apparently fought for this claim because of a belief that if the planet inhabited by humans is removed from the center of things, then human life will be less significant than previously thought—as though meaningfulness could be a matter of spatial location! [Old joke: Why is sex popular? Because it is centrally located.] Such a way of thinking is perhaps no worse than the claim one often hears as an expression of the absurdity of human life: "We are so small—such little, antlike creatures—and the universe is so very large"—as though our lives would be more meaningful if we were simply *larger* (bad news, of course, for weightwatchers!).[4] These claims may be tolerated if they are nothing more than metaphors to *express the feeling* that life is absurd, but they surely cannot literally be what *makes* it absurd if it is, or nonabsurd if it is not. Very little more, I think, can be said for the religious claim that God guarantees the meaningfulness of life by guaranteeing immortality—as though living longer would necessarily make our lives less absurd. One can, indeed, well imagine that immortality could make matters worse; an eternal inane life seems even more ridiculous than an inane life of 60–70 years duration. I am reminded here of a cartoon published a few years ago by Gahan Wilson. It shows two angels with harps sitting on clouds. One looks to the other and remarks: "Do you mean this actually goes on *forever?*" Forever is a very long time indeed, and one might well *fear* immortality because of the belief that, sooner or later, it is bound to be boring.[5] Even if this is not so, however, it is hard indeed to see how immortality could guarantee the objectivity of the kinds of values we have been discussing.

Two additional religious lines of thought are more complex and persuasive perhaps, and they are thus worth exploring in a bit more detail. One is the claim that God is the author or the guarantor of morality—of the values around which human life is to be organized—because His will *creates* morality—i.e., the good has its status as good because it is willed to be so by God. The second (and of course related) claim is that human life has meaning or purpose because God has His own purposes for our lives—i.e., that we have meaning or purpose (and thus lack absurdity) by serving His purposes.

Let us consider the second point first. Does my life become meaningful because it serves the purpose of some higher being? Well, this might at least depend on what the purposes are. Nagel expresses doubt, for example, that we would find our lives suddenly meaningful and nonabsurd if we discovered that we are being raised as *food* for some superior extraterrestrial being. (This would be rather like expecting a steer to take delight in his role in a Big Mac.) Serving others, even God, may be a wonderful thing if one *chooses* so to serve. But if the choice is not one's own—if the purposes are forced upon one—then it seems more like slavery. And this will be so no matter how important the value—i.e., no matter how more high-sounding it may seem than being raised as food. We expect objects (e.g., hammers, cars, etc.) to have purposes in this instrumental sense, not people. As Kurt Baier has remarked, most of us would be quite offended if someone walked up to us and asked, "And what are you for?"[6] To serve the purposes of another rather than one's own purposes seems, in short, *degrading*. What we want is that our lives should be meaningful *to us* (that the purposes *in* our lives should matter); and that our lives are meaningful to some other being—that he has a purpose *for* us—does not guarantee any more than that our lives are meaningful *to him*. Even this limited instrumental value will not work unless *his* life is meaningful to him or in itself. But how do we know that God's life is meaningful? Is its meaning perhaps self-guaranteed? But does the concept of "self-guarantee" make any sense; and, if it does, might it not make sense at the level of human life itself, thereby eliminating the need for any appeal to God? The questions go on and on, and thus this route seems less than promising as a way to guarantee meaning in human life.

What about the other suggestion—that God creates and guarantees the moral good by an act of will: "The good is good because God wills it." But how could goodness be created by will? (Plato's puzzle in *Euthyphro*: "Is the good good because God loves it, or does God love it because it is good?") That is, what is it about God that makes Him able to create goodness; his *power* perhaps? Surely not, for this could at most make God a kind of cosmic policeman enforcing the law (His rules) through terror and appeals to self-interest, but not necessarily creating or even acting in accord with the moral good. Indeed, if anything, the whole idea of "might is right"—even at or perhaps especially at the cosmic level—may easily appear morally disgusting. The philosopher Rush Rhees has written on this as follows:

Is the reason for not worshipping the devil instead of God that God is stronger than the devil? God will get you in the end, the devil will not be able to save you from his fury, and then you will be *for* it. 'Think of your future, boy, and don't throw away your chances.' What a creeping and vile sort of thing [that kind of] religion must be. . . .

Suppose you had to explain to someone who had no idea at all of religion or of what a belief in God was. Could you do it in this way?—By proving to him that there must be a first cause—a Something—and that this Something is more powerful (whatever this means) than anything else; so that you would not have been conceived or born at all but for the operation of Something, and Something might wipe out the existence of everything at any time? . . . Would he not be justified if he answered,

'What a horrible idea! Like a Frankenstein without limits, so that you cannot escape it. The most ghastly nightmare!' . . .

If my first and chief reason for worshipping God had to be a belief that a super-Frankenstein would blast me to hell if I did not, then I hope I should have the decency to tell this being, who is named Almighty God, to go ahead and blast.[7]

If it is not the power of God that creates goodness, what then might it be—His *knowledge* or even His *goodness?* But His knowledge of *what*—presumably the good, of course—and His goodness *by what standard?* If God is Himself properly called good, then surely there must be some standard of goodness, independent of God, whereby we evaluate Him as good. But if we already have this independent standard, then the appeal to God becomes redundant—i.e., without explanatory or justification work to do.

Now this has, of course, been an admittedly superficial survey of some very complex issues. But I hope enough has been said to make you at least skeptical that the idea of a good or meaningful life can be guaranteed by a religious postulate of God. Logically, it simply looks as though it will not work. Thus the fear that the progress of science (e.g., evolutionary biology) will undermine the belief in God and thus the rational foundation of morality is, at least with respect to the issue of morality, unfounded. The belief in God never did rationally establish morality in the first place, and thus its abandonment can hardly leave morality in any worse logical shape than it is already. Nietzsche's proclamation that "God is dead" is thus not quite the big deal that many (e.g., existentialists such as Albert Camus[8]) have taken it to be.

But if a religious foundation for ethics will not work, what then will—some secular alternative perhaps, something perhaps to be gleaned from nonreligious or antireligious moral philosophy? Here, too, I am inclined to think that the answer is again *no;* for if a religious value such as "doing God's will" will not guarantee meaningfulness, it is hard to see how some secular value (e.g., promoting the welfare of mankind, or the state, or oneself, or—a point to be stressed later on—the future of the human species) will fare any better. Such appeals will also be open to the same logical problem—namely, a dependence upon postulated values that lie beyond the possibility of rational proof. The upshot, then, is simply this: *Nothing* works; and thus there is one very real sense in which human life *is* absurd. The things that matter to us the most really cannot be proven to be of value.

Suppose with me for a moment that this is so. How should we *respond* to it? Well, as a first note, one should not do anything either rash or heroic (e.g., commit suicide or strike poses of defiance). After all, there is a bright side to all of this. We only can have absurd lives because we act with serious purpose and because we are rational enough to be able to think about the justification of what we do. We can "transcend ourselves in thought" to use a high-sounding phrase; and, so far as we know, we are the only animal capable of this and thus capable of absurdity. (A salamander cannot have an absurd life because it cannot have an intellectual view of its life.) We could, of course, avoid absurdity in life by eliminating these rather fascinating human capacities (e.g., by having ourselves lobotomized), but that would seem to be a rather high price to pay simply to avoid sailing upon a sea of uncertainty. And if we set out *seriously* to do this (or to cultivate a mystic's indifference to worldly seriousness, or to commit suicide, or to shake, with Camus, a heroic fist at this indifferent universe), we would show that we had not understood our own lesson. For if *nothing* matters, then *these gestures do not matter either!* The novelist John Barth writes as follows:

To realize that nothing makes any final difference is overwhelming; but if one goes no farther and becomes a saint, a cynic, or a suicide on principle, one hasn't reasoned completely. The truth is that nothing makes any difference, including that truth. Hamlet's question is, absolutely, meaningless.[9]

Let me now pause to summarize what I have claimed to this point: Religious myths may be elaborate, indeed even beautiful and traditionally rich, ways of *expressing* that one *finds* life meaningful, that one is able to go on from day to day in pretty much the same way that human beings generally go on. As in the myth of the fall in the Garden of Eden and its poignant revelation of the sting of lost innocence[10], they may also illustrate moral paradoxes or dramatize in an illuminating way some things that in a sense we knew all along. But so, too, may certain secular or atheistic traditions (e.g., the writings of the Stoics, Spinoza, or Nietzsche). What none of these can do, however, is *prove* the value of any of the commitments they exemplify. Their value—and it can be considerable—*is just the exemplification*. But if someone is genuinely skeptical about the values exemplified, these intellectual accounts, whether secular or religious, will not bring him around. And if he has lost his ability to go on in life in some normal way, these accounts will not give it back to him. For what, at one level, could be more *obvious* than that kindness is better than cruelty and that realizing the potentials in oneself are more important than letting oneself slide into sloth and despair. But if one really doubts this or has simply come to feel this way, how could you *argue* him out of the position? What value is more plausible than these values such that you could use it to prove them?—the importance of doing God's will? (as though this is more obvious than the importance of kindness), or the importance of the welfare of the state? (as though this is more obvious than that fulfilling oneself is worthwhile). These just will not work, and the reason for this is, I think, rather profound—namely, that when human life breaks down at this basic level, when one simply cannot go on in a way one finds meaningful, the problem is *not intellectual* at all and thus cannot be solved by *theories* (religious or secular). The person who simply cannot see the point of going on is not in that position because he does not have a *reason* for going on (what would that be?), but because he does not *feel* like going on and has lost his sense that, as Noel Coward noted, there is nothing else to do with human life but live it.

This is a difficult point (and clearly goes beyond the mere summary I had promised), and so I shall close this chapter by elaborating a bit upon its nature and history: There is a dominant rationalist tradition in philosophy, starting with Plato, that seeks to regard the basic problems in human life as intellectual in character. This tradition, picked up and modified by the early Church Fathers, has become a part of the dominant rational theology of our culture.[11] This tradition exalts the intellect or reason and regards our emotional or passionate nature—our "animal nature" as it is sometimes called—as dangerous, debased, and always in need of rational control. The dominant metaphor in this tradition is the conflict between the soul and body (or, as James Joyce called it, the conflict between soul and bawdy). So long as we control our passions by living a life dominated by values that reason can justify, our lives are meaningful. Otherwise they are absurd, even brutelike. We find a secularization of this outlook in such moral philosophies as that of Immanuel Kant.

If you are a member of this tradition and are charmed or dominated by this way of thinking, what is your reaction going to be to the realization that the reasons or theories you have accepted to found the values of your life (be they religious or secular) are intellectually bankrupt? You are going, of course, to expect the coherence of human life and civilization, and thus your own life, to disintegrate. But, of course, *they do not!* Things go on pretty much as before, all your initial fears to the contrary. Most people (you included!) still go about the business of living as before—no better in their own self-realization or their treatment of others, certainly, but not perceptibly worse either.

What could be the explanation of this? The answer is, I think, obvious: The ability to go from day to day, to live a reasonably coherent and moral life, never depended upon any intellectual theory in the first place; and the belief that it did was simply a philosopher's or theologian's myth. Our unjustly maligned "animal nature"—our passions and patterns of evolved habitual behavior—keeps us together through shared values and commitments and will continue to do so even at the loss of a covering intellectual rationale. When Hume claimed that "reason is and ought only to be the slave of the passions,"[12] he may have overstated the case. But his insight was a valuable corrective to the dominant tradition of rationalism or intellectualism; a tradition marvelously put in its place by George Eliot in *Middlemarch* when she writes:

Excuse me there. If you go upon arguments, they are never wanting, when a man has no constancy of mind. My father never changed, and he preached plain moral sermons without argument, and was a good man— few better. When you get me a good man out of arguments, I will get you a good dinner with reading you the cookery-book. That's my opinion, and I think anybody's stomach will bear me out.[13]

Perhaps it would be helpful to think of this issue in evolutionary terms: How long would our species have survived if the actions required for survival (and, for a species such as ours, these acts will include those that constitute *culture*) had awaited indubitable intellectual theories? Not *very* long, certainly. The idea that people would remain inactive and uncommitted until a provable theory to justify their actions and commitments came along is, viewed in these terms, simply too comical to take seriously. Thus no matter how much intellectual skepticism may give us momentary disquiet, our evolved passionate nature saves us from letting such skepticism take over permanently and bring the activities and commitments of our life to a standstill. The philosopher David Hume, himself a total skeptic concerning the possibility of rationally justifying anything, put the point as follows in a famous passage from his *Treatise of Human Nature*:

Most fortunately it happens, that since reason is incapable of dispelling these clouds, nature herself suffices to that purpose, and cures me of this philosophical melancholy and delirium, either by relaxing this bent of mind, or by some avocation, and lively impression of my senses, which obliterate all these chimeras. I dine, I play a game of backgammon, I converse, and am merry with my friends; and when after three or four hours' amusement, I would return to these speculations, they appear so cold, and strain'd, and ridiculous, that I cannot find in my heart to enter into them any farther.[14]

Hume's idea of "nature sufficing" is an important one that I wish I had space to explore in much greater detail. Even given my limitations of space, however, I must say at least a little bit more about it because it provides valuable intellectual background for some of the ideas to be explored later in this book. In order to be as efficient as possible about the matter, let me indulge in a bit of tasteless exhibitionism and simply quote from myself. The passage is from an essay written a few years ago in which I explored Hume's reasons for rejecting the model of a social contract in political theory. According to Hume, the model rests upon a fundamentally mistaken assumption—namely, that human beings could, at a given time, come together and rationally plan the rules and structures of a workable society (all this without a history and without any developed social life or expectations). Hume regards this model as intellectually ludicrous and, if used to justify rebellion, politically dangerous. I wrote:

Hume would say that [rationalistic social contract theory], noble as it sounds, grows out of a fundamentally wrongheaded way of thinking about social institutions—namely, that they are or could be a product of rational or intellectual design. This is the way it is made to appear in philosophy books and in the rhetoric of revolutionaries, but it is not the way the social and political world really is. A few aspects may be changed here and there (and often should be), but the social and political fabric itself in which such changes take place (and even the *language* at our disposal to talk about the suggested changes)[15] are the products of a process of undesigned social evolution over the inheritance of which we have no control. Christian Bay has called Hume a precursor of Darwin in the field of ethics and social philosophy, and this claim strikes me as fundamentally correct.[16] As we know from Part VIII of the *Dialogues Concerning Natural Religion,* Hume clearly anticipated the doctrine of natural selection as an explanatory mechanism for biological evolution (thus dispensing with the need for teleological explanations),[17] and I believe that these same patterns of thought are to be found in his moral and social writings. As Friedrich von Hayek has put it: "Hume undertakes to show that certain characteristics of modern society which we prize are dependent on conditions which were not created in order to bring about these results, yet are nevertheless their indispensable presuppositions."[18] In Hume, this line of thought is most clearly developed in the section of the *Treatise* "Of the Origin of Justice and Property." There Hume argues that individual men are naturally vulnerable (and thus with doubtful potential for survival) and can therefore survive only if ways are evolved to allow them to live together and thus gain collective strength in communities. Obstacles to such social unions are individual selfishness, the narrow bounds of human understanding (i.e., limited knowledge), and scarcity of the objects of desire. Ways to overcome these obstacles *had* to develop (otherwise humanity would not have survived) and the primary mechanism that evolved was the *largely unquestioned obedience to certain rules of conduct.* Which rules?—those with utility or survival value. These rules (because of the very limitations of men noted above) must evolve by a natural selection process and cannot be the result of rational human design: "To balance a large state of society, whether monarchial or republican, on general laws, is a work of so great difficulty, that no human genius, however comprehensive, is able by the mere dint of reason and reflection, to effect it. The judgements of many must unite in this work: Experience must guide their labour: Time must bring it to perfection: And the feeling of inconveniences must correct the mistakes, which they inevitably fall into, in their first trials and experiments" ("Of the Rise and Progress of the Arts and Sciences").[19]

Hume, of course, is not alone in his attack on rationalism in ethics. Such attacks go back in philosophy at least as far as Aristotle and continue into the present day. What is special about Hume,

and what distinguishes him from many other opponents of rationalism, is that he sees the flaw of rationalism as part of a more
general flaw present in many accounts of morality—namely, the
tendency to see morality as primarily a cognitive enterprise, an
enterprise that produces universal objective knowledge. Moral
sense theorists, for example, are not rationalists, but they sometimes claim to get ethical certainty out of experience or intuition.
Not so with Hume. In ethics, as in epistemology, Hume should be
understood not merely as an antirationalist, but as a *skeptic*—one
who regards the basic claims of ethics as fundamentally unprov-
able (either by reason or experience). We *feel* certain about various
ethical propositions, and we act on them as if we had certain
knowledge. This, however, is simply a *fact about our nature* and not
a kind of justification. The appeal to our nature ("nature suffices")
is not another kind of justification; it is rather an explanation of
how we manage to go on in the absence of justification.

Those in company with Hume here are a smaller number,
particularly among philosophers. We find such views in Marx and
Freud, but, since these writers were concerned with morality only
tangentially to their primary interests, they have left us no developed accounts. The only other systematic philosophical account of
moral skepticism (prior to the twentieth century[20]) at all comparable in scope and power to Hume's is that presented by the much
misunderstood and much maligned and much ignored nineteenth
century German philosopher Friedrich Nietzsche. On the surface
no two thinkers could appear more different than the calm and
witty Hume and the rhetorically violent and sometimes mad
Nietzsche. Yet, once one gets below the surface rhetoric, there are
enormous similarities between the views of the two men. Like
Hume, Nietzsche mounts an attack on the pretensions of moral
philosophy to deliver provable moral knowledge.[21] Also, like
Hume, Nietzsche suggests that morality is best understood as an
outgrowth of certain fundamental features of our human nature
("human all too human"). Hume is rather cheerful about it all, of
course; whereas Nietzsche vacillates between rage and messianic-
prophetic hopefulness. But the logical core of the two views is
quite similar in that both see our morality in terms of its primitive
psychological origins—Hume in terms of generally attractive features (e.g., sympathy) and Nietzsche in terms of generally unat-

tractive features (e.g., resentment). Both men clearly think that knowing the causal origins of our moral views is important to philosophical understanding; it is not simply a scientific inquiry that the philosopher can safely ignore. Nietzsche writes:

Fortunately I learned early to separate theological prejudice from moral prejudice and ceased to look for the origin of evil *behind* the world. A certain amount of historical and philological schooling, together with an inborn fastidiousness of taste in respect to psychological questions in general, soon transformed my problem into another one: under what conditions did man devise these value judgments good and evil? *and what value do they themselves possess?* Have they hitherto hindered or furthered human prosperity? Are they a sign of distress, of impoverishment, or the degeneration of life? Or is there revealed in them, on the contrary, the plenitude, force, and will of life, its courage, certainty, future? . . . We need a *critique* of moral values, *the value of these values themselves must first be called in question*—and for that there is needed a knowledge of the conditions and circumstances in which they grew, under which they evolved and changed.[22]

This summary discussion of Hume and Nietzsche has been admittedly superficial and distorted. I put it here, however, not to provide education in the history of philosophy, but to suggest a point ultimately relevant to Darwin's views on ethics and to contemporary sociobiology: These scientific accounts should not be viewed as isolated, but should, instead, be seen as part of a tradition in moral philosophy that includes such powerful thinkers as Hume and Nietzsche. Why does this matter? Because philosophers might not be so inclined to reject sociobiology out of hand if they see it in terms of some of their own traditions.

Suppose that one agrees that Hume, Darwin, Nietzsche, Freud, Marx, and Wilson do all have this in common: a belief that a study of the causal *origins* of moral judgments is central to a philosophical understanding of morality, central because, once we come to accept certain accounts of the origin of the judgments, we will see that we are required to give up venerable moral theories and the pretensions of traditional moral philosophy. Suppose that one agrees that this is the common claim. One might still want to dismiss this claim (and all the listed thinkers) out of hand because of the conviction that the core belief that unites them all is silly, even fallacious. In introductory logic we learn not to commit the *genetic fallacy*—the fallacy of believing that the causal origin of a belief affects the truth or reasonableness of that belief. The Nazis, for example, were quite stupid in rejecting the contents of psychoanalytic theory because its founder (Freud) was a Jew. And Freud himself (so the argument sometimes goes) was comparably stupid in his attack on religion. Even if he is correct in claiming that people believe in God because they cannot give up certain infantile wish-fulfillment fantasies, it does not follow from this that the proposition "God exists" is false or unreasonable to believe. Thus if Freud thought he was undermining religion by his theory of causal origins, he was simply mistaken and was merely committing the genetic fallacy.

At a certain level, the above makes good sense; for there is a certain context in which there is such a thing as a genetic fallacy and, in that context, we should not commit it. However, the matter is considerably more complex and deeper than those who argue as above would suggest. For example, sometimes we know it to be the case that false or unreasonable beliefs are highly correlated with persons of a certain type, and we are therefore quite properly inclined to exclude (in a court of law) testimony from a person who is drunk or under the influence of drugs. When we do this very reasonable thing, we certainly should not be charged with committing a genetic fallacy. Or consider Wesley Salmon's discussion of scientific "cranks."[23] According to Salmon, these are persons who usually reject established science, are ignorant of the science they reject, publish and present their claims outside the normal channel of reviewed scientific publications, regard opposition to their theories as persecution and bigotry, and often have a religious, political, or moral basis for their doctrines. Surely we commit no fallacy (but are instead being reasonable) if we conclude that a "scientific" theory propounded by a person who has these characteristics is very probably (though not certainly) false. The appeal to origins is thus not automatically irrelevant in assessing the reasonableness of a view or theory.

Returning to morality and religion, let us think again about the question of origins. We all, I think, tend to operate with a strong bias in favor of commonly accepted beliefs. That is, if a belief is very widely held, our inclination is to think that there is probably something true in the belief and that the burden of proof lies on the person who would challenge the belief. The belief in God, the belief in objective morality, and the belief that the two are connected is a belief cluster widely held in our culture. Thus we are initially inclined to take it quite seriously and to regard as profound (not pretentious) those philosophical and theological theories that involve or presuppose that cluster. But suppose Freud shows that religious belief is caused simply by wish fulfillment. Suppose Nietzsche shows that Christian morality is to be explained as the sublimation of hate, envy, and resentment. Suppose that Marx persuades us that the morality of property rights is generated and reinforced as a mechanism whereby one social class oppresses another. If we come to believe these accounts of causal origins, then surely, at the very least, we will abandon our bias in favor of the conventional wisdom on these matters and will not automatically regard as profound (but may even start to regard as pretentious) those theories in philosophy that are smug and complacent about the values and beliefs we (given our new perspective) can now see are open to doubt. This is the sense in which an inquiry into origins is philosophically respectable and even important; and this is the sense in which I see Hume, Darwin, Nietzsche, and Wilson as united in a common endeavor.

This pretty well finishes everything I have to say in this first chapter. I have followed Hume's example and have attempted to use the rational methods of philosophy in order to undermine some of the rational pretensions of philosophy (and those of its embarrassing poor relation of rational theology); and thus it may seem that I have been a traitor to my discipline. But I do not think so. Rational proof, after all, is not everything, even in philosophy. And sometimes, as I have suggested here, it is not much at all. Sometimes it is instructive and valuable, I think, simply to attempt to *understand* and to *exemplify* some things—some values, some patterns of thought, some limitations of thought, some features of our nature. Such at any rate has been my attempt and hope in this chapter, and I shall leave it to the reader to determine if it has been instructive and valuable.

What, then, comes next? In this chapter, I have suggested, in the most vague and general terms, that an evolutionary perspective on morality will be useful in understanding its nature and foundations. In order to answer the question of just *how* useful such a perspective will actually be, it will be necessary to consider such accounts in detail. Such consideration will begin in the next two chapters where I explore the thoughts of Charles Darwin—his general evolutionary theory (in Chapter 2) and his theory of the origin of morality or, as he himself puts it, the *moral sense* (in Chapter 3).

Notes

1. I am not at all confident that this chapter contains even one truly original idea, and so it is, I think, best to view this chapter as simply the presentation and elaboration of some philosophical ideas that have had a great influence upon my own thinking—a set of "variations upon an unoriginal theme" if you will. Brooding over the entire enterprise is David Hume, a philosopher whose writings increasingly strike me as the most profound in the history of philosophy. To a certain lesser extent, the influence of the writings on moral philosophy (especially *Beyond Good and Evil* and *The Genealogy of Morals*) by Friedrich Nietzsche is also present. Moving to the contemporary philosophical scene, I must mention my debt to and admiration for Thomas Nagel's essay "The Absurd," *The Journal of Philosophy*, (October 21, 1971), pp. 716–27—a contemporary restatement of a generally Humean outlook on these matters.

2. Actually, the matter is a bit more complicated than I have suggested. There are really two senses of "why"—the *causal* or *explanatory* "why" and the "why" of *justification*. The former kind of "why" clearly does have a place in science; for example: "Why did he die?"/"Because of a heart attack," or "Why does smoking cause lung cancer?"/"Because chemicals in cigarette smoke cause genetic mutation." Of course, if Hume and his followers are correct, these causal "whys" are all reducible to statments of "how"—i.e., to statements concerning regularities of experience. Even if this is so, however, there is still a point to keeping alive the scientific notion of "why" at the level of ordinary discourse in order to keep people from being mistakenly tempted to believe that science never really explains anything. The "whys" with which this chapter is concerned are those of *justification*—a request for ends, goals, or purposes as *desirable values*. (This is, of course, different from the metaphorical sense in which, simply to describe the function of a certain part of an organism, we use in a nonevaluative sense the *language* of ends, purposes or goals. For example: "The purpose of the heart is to pump blood to the rest of the body." This is not to say that the heart *has* a purpose, but only that it can be described as *serving* a purpose.) I am grateful to Wesley Salmon for calling my attention to some serious shortcomings in an earlier account I had written on these issues. For Hume's views on causation, see *Treatise*, Book I, Part III, Sections I–VIII, XI–XII, XIV–XV; and *Enquiry*, Sections IV–VIII.

3. The analogy with Hume's views on induction is instructive here. Let us employ Carnap's distinction between internal and external questions, and let us employ the metaphor of a *game* in discussing such cognitive human activities as science, morality, etc. Within the game, there will be a rule-governed distinction between correct and incorrect "moves." Questions about this distinction will be internal questions, questions *within* the game. But there can also be questions *about* the game—e.g., is it reasonable to play it? These are external questions. Let us regard science as what might be called the "evidence game." There is a right and a wrong way to play this, a difference between good and bad inductive probabilistic arguments—e.g., testimony from gullible, uneducated persons is given less weight than testimony from objective, informed persons. (This is a kind of "internal" point Hume continually makes so well in his essay "Of Miracles.") At a certain point, however, one might want to raise a much more profound question—namely, can we rationally justify playing the inductive evidence game at all, can we demonstrate the rational superiority of that game to other competitors such as religion and magic? As Hume argues in his writings on causation, induction, and probability, the answer to this external question is *no*. The only arguments for induction are themselves inductive, and thus the supposed justification for induction is circular. This is the essence of Hume's skepticism about induction. (For Hume's skeptical views on induction, see especially *Enquiry*, Sections IV–V.)

So too, for morality. Of course, given certain commonly shared assumptions, we can distinguish between a correct and an incorrect moral justification. Things go fine and are even easy at this internal level, but when we seek to justify externally the basic assumptions presupposed in answering the internal questions, we find that we cannot do so in a noncircular way. The parallels between moral skepticism and inductive skepticism are thus quite close.

4. "Where I seem to differ from some of my friends is in attaching little importance to physical size. I don't feel the least humble before the vastness of the heavens. The stars may be large, but they cannot think or love; and these are qualities which impress me far more than size does. I take no credit for weighing nearly seventeen stone." Frank Ramsey, *The Foundations of Mathematics*, (Paterson, NJ: Littlefield, Adams, 1960), p. 291.

5. See Bernard Williams, "The Makropulos Case: Reflections on the Tedium of Immortality," in his *Problems of the Self* (Cambridge: Cambridge University Press, 1973), pp. 82–100.

6. Kurt Baier, "The Meaning of Life," The Inaugural Lecture at Canberra University College (1957).

7. Rush Rhees, *Without Answers* (London: Routledge and Kegan Paul, 1969), pp. 112–13.

8. "There is but one moral code that the absurd man can accept, the one that is not separated from God: the one that is dictated. But it so happens that he lives outside that God. . . . The certainty of a God giving meaning to life far surpasses in attractiveness the ability to behave badly

with impunity," Albert Camus, "The Absurd Man," in *The Myth of Sisyphus and other Essays*, trans. Justin O'Brien (New York: Random House, Inc., 1955), pp. 49–50.

9. John Barth, *The Floating Opera* (New York: Bantam Books, Inc., 1967), p. 246. The question, of course, is "To be, or not to be?"

10. See Herbert Morris, "Lost Innocence," in his *On Guilt and Innocence* (Berkeley: University of California Press, 1976), pp. 139–61.

11. By "rational theology" I mean something similar to what Hume meant by "natural theology"—i.e., the attempt to *prove*, in a quasi-scientific way, the basic claims of religion and to then prove (i.e., derive) moral claims from this religious basis. There is much theology that does not have this character and will thus be unaffected by my criticisms. Representatives of such theology may legitimately plead "Not guilty!" to the charge of attempting to prove religious and moral claims in this way. Such writers as D. Z. Phillips, for example, do not like to see religion play pseudo-science any more than I do.

12. *Treatise*, Book II, Part III, Sec. III.

13. Chap. 17 (Mrs. Farebrother is speaking).

14. *Treatise*, Book I, Part IV, Sec. VII.

15. Hume no doubt would have liked the following remark by J. L. Austin about words who claimed that they embody "all the distinctions men have found worth drawing, and the connexions they have found worth marking, in the lifetimes of many generations: these surely are likely to be more numerous, more sound, since they have stood up to the long test of the survival of the fittest, and more subtle, at least in all ordinary and reasonably practical matters, than any that you or I are likely to think up in our armchairs of an afternoon—the most favoured alternative method," "A Plea for Excuses," *Philosophical Papers* (Oxford: Oxford University Press, 1961), p. 130.

16. *The Structure of Freedom* (Stanford: Stanford University Press, 1958), p. 33. (It is, of course, recognized that the views of Hume's contemporary Adam Smith influenced Darwin).

17. For a detailed discussion of this issue, see Chapter 2.

18. "The Legal and Political Philosophy of David Hume," *Hume*, ed. V. C. Chappel (Garden City: Doubleday & Co., 1966), p. 335. My interpretation of Hume has been greatly influenced by Hayek's work.

19. Jeffrie G. Murphy, "Hume and Kant on the Social Contract," in *Retribution, Justice and Therapy: Essays in the Philosophy of Law* (Dordrecht and Boston: D. Reidel, 1979), pp. 61–62.

20. The twentieth century meta-ethical theory of *emotivism* is instructively viewed as a continuation of Humean patterns of thought. The best book developing emotivism (and, to my mind, one of the best books written in ethics in this century) is the now sadly neglected book by Charles Stevenson, *Ethics and Language* (New Haven: Yale University Press, 1944). See also J. L. Mackie, *Ethics: Inventing Right and Wrong* (New York: Penquin, 1977) and Gilbert Harmon, *The Nature of Morality* (Oxford: Oxford University Press, 1977).

21. For reasons too boring to detail, Nietzsche tends not to like the term "skeptic." He is, however, an ethical skeptic in the same sense that Hume is.

22. *Genealogy of Morals*, Preface, Sections 3 and 6.

23. Wesley Salmon, *Logic*, Second Edition (Englewood Cliffs: Prentice-Hall, 1973), pp. 11, 96.

2

Scientific Creationism and the Darwinian Revolution

> What peculiar privilege has this little agitation of the brain which we call thought, that we must thus make it the model of the whole universe?
>
> DAVID HUME

Once upon a time the world was a comforting place in which to live, for we human beings were able to embrace a worldview that provided us with nearly endless flattery and ego gratification.[1] The whole universe, we were told, had been created by God *for us*. We had been placed at the physical and moral center so that we could act out, on center stage and before a divine audience, our individual dramas of sin and redemption. Suffering might befall us; but, if so, this would be our own fault—our failure to use the impressive gifts of free will and moral responsibility in the proper and approved way. This picture dominated Western thought throughout the Middle Ages.

With the onset of the Renaissance scientific revolution, however, it seemed as though a group of killjoys were attempting to put ugly blots upon this beautiful picture. Even more upsetting, these killjoys seemed to be able to defend their acts of defacement with powerful evidence and arguments. Copernicus rendered it plausible to believe that our earth is not even at the center of our little

31

system (the sun is)—much less at the center of the whole universe. Galileo and Newton showed how the phenomena of astronomy and physics could be explained in terms of mechanistic and deterministic causal laws, thus dispensing with the need to explain things teleologically—i.e., in terms of plans and purposes, God's or anyone else's.

What was orthodox religion to do? One option, of course, would have been simply to give up and quit, thus giving new meaning to the concept of a religious retreat. For obvious reasons, this option had little appeal. Another option was to use violence against the new science—suppress the circulation of new scientific ideas and imprison or even kill noncooperative scientists. Though this option was, alas, sometimes exercised, it did not represent the best within the religious traditions of Christianity. Thus many Christians searched instead for morally and intellectually respectable ways of dealing with the threat posed by the new science. One option adopted by the Christian philosopher and scientist René Descartes, was to adopt a position of metaphysical *dualism*—a distinction between physical body and spiritual mind (soul) as fundamentally different kinds of substance.[2] Very roughly the position of dualism said the following: The world of physical bodies is to be totally explained by deterministic science; this poses no threat to true religion, however, since true religion concerns the realm of mind, soul, or spirit. As long as this realm is conceived as fundamentally different from the physical, what is essentially important (both religiously and morally) about human beings will be insulated from any threat posed by the march of science.

As a temporary holding measure, dualism was a success. As long as religion and morality get to keep the mind and spirit (that which is essentially and importantly human), and as long as what goes on in that world is to be explained in terms of purposes (God's and our own), then what threat could be posed by a nonteleological account of external matter? According to Descartes, even all nonhuman animals could be allowed to fall under the explanatory devices of the new science. The "brutes," he claimed, are just complex machines and, like all machines, can be explained on the basis of a materialistic and deterministic worldview.

The stage is now set for the next generation of killjoys: the group of scientists beginning with Darwin and going through Freud and B. F. Skinner. Darwin eliminated religious teleological explanations from the animal world by arguing that species arose, not because God planned or created them that way, but by purely causal processes. So too, he argued, for the species *homo sapiens*. No special creative miracle is required to explain the origin of human beings. We human beings, fascinating creatures though we may be, differ from other animals (pretty fascinating themselves) less than we like to suppose. Our most impressive intellectual and moral qualities, for example, are claimed by Darwin to differ simply in degree, and not in kind, from those found in the higher mammals. Thus a good case can be made that we descended from nonhuman animals; and thus if their behavior can be explained mechanistically, then so too can ours. Deterministic psychology was thus the natural outgrowth from what Darwin started.[3] The idea that mind or spirit is really something separate from the physical body had long been challenged by philosophers (e.g., Thomas Hobbes regarded mind as brain atoms in motion), but the biology and psychology that started with Darwin seemed to provide hard evidence for what had previously been just a philosophical speculation. Bad news again, it seemed, for the world of orthodox religion.

Now there are many ways (some of them obscure, some of them quite clever) in which one might attempt to save religion from this onslaught of scientific discovery: interpret religion metaphorically or symbolically, talk of faith and mystery instead of evidence and reason, insist that religion is mainly ethics ("ultimate concern") and not metaphysics, regard religion and science as two radically different ways of *talking* about the world (language games or forms of life) that are compatible since we talk for different purposes in the two cases, or even use Humean skepticism on behalf of religion—i.e., recall that Hume mounted a powerful skeptical case against induction (the basic methodology of science) and thus (perhaps unwittingly) showed that the person who rejects science cannot be proven irrational for so doing.[4] Religious persons can even joyfully *embrace* such scientific theories as evolution by natural selection by regarding this mechanism as God's way of effecting His purposes in the world.

The above, of course, are all various strategies of avoidance.

There is one way of interpreting religion, however, that involves challenging certain scientific claims head on—attacking those claims with a vigor and directness that is (depending on your point of view) courageous or stupid. On this interpretation of religion, some religious claims are *themselves empirical scientific claims*—claims that represent, according to their defenders, *better science* (i.e., a set of better confirmed hypotheses) than what is offered by nonreligious or antireligious science. This way of interpreting religion was called Natural Religion or Natural Theology in the eighteenth and nineteenth centuries, and our present-day variant of it is called Scientific Creationism.[5]

Natural Religion, Natural Theology, and Scientific Creationism

According to Christian orthodoxy, God (an infinitely powerful, wise, and good being) created the entire universe *ex nihilo* in order to serve certain plans or purposes of His own. (The story of this is in Genesis.) He created, in a short span of time, all the physical matter in the universe and all living forms, including human beings. These latter creatures were given *souls* and were thereby rendered quite special. All species of life forms were created at the outset (by acts of special creation) and no new species have since arisen. (If some of the original life forms have ceased to exist, this is because God allowed them to be destroyed in Noah's flood.) It is our task as human beings to accept this world as given to us and to live out the duties God has prescribed for us. We are to believe what we are told by God and are not to seek alternative accounts through alternative routes to knowledge—one point of the story of the fall, where Adam and Eve (and all their descendents) suffer from having disobeyed God and eaten the fruit of the tree of knowledge.

There are, of course, many ways in which one can interpret the above story—as a myth, for example, or as something to be accepted entirely on faith. Those who practice Natural Religion, Natural Theology, or Scientific Creationism, however, interpret it, or at least large parts of it, in the following way: The story is literally true, not metaphor or myth, and may be regarded as a highly confirmed scientific hypothesis—i.e., it does not have to be accepted totally on faith. To say that it is a scientific hypothesis is to say that it is the sort of claim that can be established (or refuted) on the basis of empirical evidence. To say that it is a highly confirmed scientific hypothesis is to say that, given the evidence available to us, it is the most reasonable hypothesis to hold concerning the origin of the universe and life. (Contemporary Scientific Creationists sometimes offer a weaker claim: The special creation hypothesis is, given the available evidence, at least as well confirmed as the Darwinian hypothesis, and thus each should be given equal time in teaching and discussion.[6])

How might one attempt to use empirical evidence to support a claim of special supernatural creation? David Hume considered and rejected such an attempt in his little essay "Of Miracles" (Section X of his 1748 *Enquiry Concerning Human Understanding*) where he examined the argument from *miracles* for the existence of God. The argument from miracles goes like this:

(1) A miracle is, by definition, a violation of all known laws of nature and is thus an event that, given those laws, could not have occurred.

(2) But miracles have occurred. We have ample evidence for their occurrence from the scriptures—e.g., Christ changing water into wine, walking on water, and raising Lazarus from the dead (events that violate all known laws of nature).

(3) Since miracles have occurred, and since their occurrence cannot be explained naturally in terms of known scientific laws, it is reasonable to suppose that they are to be explained *supernaturally*, by divine intervention into the natural world.

(4) Since the Christian God is the best candidate we have for divine intervener, it is reasonable to suppose, on the basis of the above evidence, that this God exists.

On the surface, this argument has plausibility. Hume suggests, however, that the argument is in fact rotten to the core. For two questions must be raised about an argument of this nature that attempts to provide an explanation for supposedly observed occurrences: (1) Is the explanation offered even *possible*—i.e., *could* it be the explanation for the event in question? (2) If it is a possible explanation, is it likely or probably the actual explanation?

Now Hume believes that the explanation offered in the above pattern of argument (the argument from miracles to God) is not even a possible explanation; it is a pseudo-explanation and thus, if offered as science, is pseudo-science. Something offered as an explanation for the production of some event *B* by another event *A* will be rationally acceptable only if we can understand or render intelligible to ourselves the *mechanism* whereby *A* could produce *B*. But we do not understand any mechanism of supernatural causation—all our causal judgments being learned as relations between natural events.[7] Thus the concept of cause here is a phony, a mystery. But to explain in terms of a mystery is not to explain at all. Though we say things such as "God caused the world—created it from nothing," we literally do not know what we mean when we say this. It is simply a fancy way of masking our ignorance, "God caused the world" telling us nothing more than "I do not know what caused the world."

Let us suppose that this problem could be overcome; that supernatural causation could be a possible explanation for those exciting events reported as miracles in the scriptures. Would it be the most probable explanation? Hume answers *no* to this question. He asks us to recall that the evidence in favor of the occurrence of miracles is historical testimony, and the testimony available is of the worst possible kind: that of ignorant and gullible people who very likely would have succumed to the common human desire to believe the fantastical and weird (perhaps because the mundane seems boring).[8] Anticipating P. T. Barnum's insight that there is a sucker born every minute, Hume asks us to consider which of the following two hypotheses is, given all available evidence, the more probable:

H1: The laws of physics were violated.

H2: A group of primitive, ignorant, and no doubt gullible people made a mistake in reporting or interpreting what they saw.

Surely, says Hume, H2 is considerably more probable than H1. Indeed, he notes, what better evidence could we have that an event probably did not occur than that the very description of that event involves a violation of a law of nature? Surely it would be prudent here to remain agnostic about the claim that these fantastical events occurred. (We cannot give special weight to this testimony as *revelation*, of course, because that would beg the very question at issue. Reports of miracles are being used to provide evidence for the existence of God, and to regard a report as a revelation is already to assume the existence of God.) Even if we come to believe that such events occurred, there are more reasonable options to consider than an immediate jump to the mystery of supernatural causation. These are: (1) honestly admit ignorance of the causation for these events, (2) look for new scientific laws that will explain the event in question, or even (3) regard God as a physical being who causes things naturalistically. (If God is conceived physically, of course, this raises the embarrassing problem of where is He?) There is, no doubt, an honorable place for the ideas of mystery and faith within religion, but appeals to mystery and faith must be given up when religion goes forth as science—one of the many prices religion pays for playing in this particular ballpark, a ballpark where its destiny may always be to lose.

The primary empirical argument for the existence of God the Creator in Hume's (and Darwin's) day was not the argument from miracles; it was rather the *Argument from Design*. This argument had one great advantage over the argument from miracles in that it did not rely on the suspect evidence of (possibly faulty) historical testimony. Its evidence was open to all—to be found in the observable natural world around us. Though Hume is the most famous critic of the argument from design, he also gave it one of its most persuasive statements. This statement occurs in his *Dialogues Concerning Natural Religion* (1779) and is expressed by the character Cleanthes. (The character Philo expresses the position of skepticism and the character Demea expresses some unclear combination of faith, mystery, and authority.) So well does Hume articulate the various positions that scholars still disagree about which character represents his own views. I obviously see him mainly in Philo, but there is plenty of support for the view that he is to be found in one of the other characters. Be that as it may, here is Cleanthes' statement of the argument from design:

Look round the world: Contemplate the whole and every part of it: You will find it to be nothing but one great machine, subdivided into an infinite number of lesser machines, which again admit of subdivisions, to a degree beyond what human senses and faculties can trace and explain.

All these various machines, and even their most minute parts, are adjusted to each other with an accuracy, which ravishes into admiration all men, who have ever contemplated them. The curious adapting of means to ends, throughout all nature, resembles exactly, though it much exceeds, the productions of human contrivance; of human design, thought, wisdom, and intelligence. Since therefore the effects resemble each other, we are led to infer, by all the rules of analogy, that the causes also resemble; and that the Author of nature is somewhat similar to the mind of man; though possessed of much larger faculties, proportioned to the grandeur of the work, which he has executed (Part II).

To use the analogy later employed by William Paley:[9] If we found a watch on the beach, we would never suppose that it simply formed itself from molecules by chance. We would instead say that it had been made by human design and left there by human agency. But surely the universe is a much more complex and impressive machine than a mere watch, and thus it is even more fantastical to suppose that it and the remarkable objects and creatures it contains could have arisen by chance. It is even more absurd, for example, to suppose that the *human eye* could have arisen by chance than to suppose a watch could have. No, there must have been intelligent design at work—creative planning and power beyond any human scope. Such planning and power could only be supernatural and divine, the work of God.

The argument as sketched above does, I think, have a powerful intuitive appeal. The universe is rather impressive, and it is hard to imagine something so impressive arising by chance. However, as Hume seeks to show, the argument will not bear close scrutiny. The passages given to Philo in the *Dialogues* represent one of the most careful search-and-destroy operations in the history of philosophy—a logical, epistemological, and rhetorical *tour de force*. Brief summary cannot do it justice, and so all I shall attempt to do here is give the highlights of Philo's (and, making my own choice clear, what I shall henceforth call Hume's) case against the argument from design. Basically Hume's attack takes this form: The design argument does not work; and, even if it did work, it would not prove what the orthodox Christian wants to get out of it. It fails to work for two reasons. First, it employs at some crucial point that same mysterious notion of supernatural causation criticized in discussing the argument from miracles. Second, it is an analogical argument and unfortunately builds its case upon a very *weak* analogy; what it seeks to explain can be explained just as well or better by alternative hypotheses. But suppose it did work—i.e., suppose the analogy between a human contrivance (e.g., a watch) and the universe was, in fact, not weak but strong. This would by analogy (the principle that like effects have like causes) require that we hold a very unattractively anthropomorphic view of the divinity, something traditional Christians would not like at all. Having seen the general nature of Hume's attack, let us have a look at some of the details.

The structure of the argument from design, remember, is that of an analogical argument, and Hume is well aware that there is nothing wrong in principle with such arguments and that indeed they have an important place in scientific discovery and explanation. The structure of an analogical argument is basically this:[10]

(1) Objects $O_1, O_2, O_3 \ldots O_n$ have properties $P_2, P_3, P_4, \ldots P_n$ in common.
(2) Objects $O_2, O_3, \ldots O_n$ have property P_1.
Therefore:
(3) It is *probable* that O_1 has property P_1.

Here is an example where such an argument could be put to rational use: "We have previously noted six diseases having certain characteristic symptoms (fever, chills, vomiting, etc.) and have discovered, through examination of blood samples, that these diseases are caused by microorganisms. The seventh disease we have now just noted has very similar symptoms, and thus it is probably caused by a microorganism too. This is at least the best first bet, and so let's take a blood sample and start looking for a microorganism."

It should be obvious that the strength of analogical arguments of the form above is a function of several factors. The greater the number of objects surveyed in $O_2 \ldots O_n$ having properties $P_1 \ldots P_n$, the more probable is the conclusion; and the greater the number of properties included in $P_2 \ldots P_n$ that the objects $O_1 \ldots O_n$ have in common, the more probable the conclusion. Putting this as simply as possible: the bigger the sample, the more probable the conclusion; the stronger the analogy (i.e., the more properties in common) the more probable the conclusion. (Six diseases is a more valuable base than two, but fourteen would be even better; three symptoms in common is better than one, but seven would be even better—i.e., make the diseases more similar or analogous.) Factors obviously decreasing the probability of the conclusion are these: objects having $P_2 \ldots P_n$ but *not* having P_1 (the more of these, the less probable the conclusion), and a conclusion that makes an overly strong claim (the stronger the claim made by the conclusion, the weaker the probability of the conclusion, given the same evidential base). If three of the six diseases having similar symptoms were caused by tumor spread (and not by microorganisms), then the argument for microorganism causation of the seventh would not be as compelling as if all six similar diseases had been found to originate with microorganisms. Consider also how degree of strength of the conclusion (i.e., the scope or ambition of its claim) affects the probability of the result. Given the same noted evidential base for all conclusions, that the disease is caused by some microorganism is more probable than that it is caused by a bacterium instead of a virus, which is in turn more probable than that it is caused by a specifically named bacterium (the tuberculosis bacillus, for example) rather than any other bacterium or virus. The point is actually quite simple: The less you claim, the less you have to prove.

Given this brief background on analogical arguments and their assessment, let us turn to the design argument for the existence of God the Creator. Using the structure outlined above, James Cornman puts the argument in the following way:

We can put Cleanthes' argument into the form of analogical arguments that we have previously discussed by letting O_1 = the universe, $O_2 \ldots O_n$ = various kinds of machines, P_1 = the property of having an intelligent designer and creator and $P_2 \ldots P_n$ = various properties O_1 has in common with $O_2 \ldots O_n$. If we pick for an example of a machine a watch as used by another defender of the argument, William Paley, we can point out several properties in common. A watch has gears which revolve in a certain orderly way on certain axes, some of which affect others so as to cause the regular ticking off of the seconds, minutes, and hours. Similarly, we can observe the moon revolving around the earth and the earth revolving on its axis, and also around the sun, in a certain orderly way so as to cause the regular rising and falling of the tides and the regular coming of day and night. The earth, moon, and sun in their various relationships to each other produce a regular temporal procession just as do the gears of a watch in their various relationships. And because a watch has property P_1 (that is, has an intelligent designer and creator), so also, most probably, does the earth and the rest of the universe.[11]

Hume's main attack on the argument thus put is an attempt to develop serious problems for the analogy at the argument's core. He first notes that there are numerous objects having properties P_2 . . . P_n (and thus like the universe in the relevant respects) that may *not* have the property of P_1 (an intelligent designer or creator), but that may have arisen as the causal product of nonintelligent causal forces: vegetable reproduction, animal reproduction, and instinct. The intricate systematic order of a tree is at least as impressive as that of a watch, but we need not postulate intelligent design to account for this order; the causal factors of seed, moist earth, and sunlight will do this explanatory job just fine. Similarly with a puppy or a spider web: beautiful order and harmony, yes, but no necessarily intelligent design—the former being the result of animal reproduction, the latter the result of instinct. Thus, perhaps the universe is more like a big carrot, a puppy, or a spider web than it is like a watch. Given the evidence available (not much), not one of these claims is any more or less plausible than the others. The initial plausibility of the design argument is generated by its presentation in the context of a false dichotomy: either the universe is the result of intelligent creation *or* it is the result of chance. If we find it hard to believe that the order and harmonious adaptation of structure to function we find in the world is the result of mere chance, of randomness, then we are likely to buy intelligent creation as the true explanation. However, once we realize that there are causal ways of producing order other than by chance, we see that the possibilities for avoiding the conclusion of the design argument are enormous. To explain by vegetable reproduction, animal reproduction, or instinct is *not* to explain by chance, but neither is it to explain by intelligent creation. And yet it does seem to explain even a very high level of systematic order— plants, animals, spider webs, and honeycombs being pretty damned impressive.[12] Thus to assume that the antiteleologist is forced to say of everything that "it is just a matter of chance" is a gross distortion.

Even the appeal to chance, however, if properly stated and

qualified, is not as ridiculous as Paley would have us suppose. Remember his discussion of the human eye—so marvelously adapted in its structure for its function of allowing us to attain orientation within our environment. According to Paley, it is just as ludicrous to imagine this complex organ arising by chance as it would be to imagine a watch forming itself by chance on the beach. This is perhaps correct if we think of the eye being formed all at once as one big random event. But consider the Darwinian account of natural selection to be explored in detail in the next section of this chapter: Small variations (a single light-sensitive skin cell, perhaps) arise by chance in organisms.[13] If this variation gives the organism survival and reproductive advantage, the organism will be more likely to win out in the struggle for existence over those organisms not so advantaged. (This is all it really means to say that the organism is "naturally selected.") So now we have a few organisms with a light-sensitive cell on the outer skin. Suppose that (again by chance) one or some of these light-sensitive cells replicate—starting to form a cluster of light-sensitive cells (a proto-eye perhaps). Organisms having these structures will now be advantaged over those of their fellows having only one light-sensitive skin cell, and those with the proto-eye will be more likely to survive and reproduce. Given that the process being described has millions and millions of years in which to work, it is not at all ludicrous to imagine that very complex adaptive structures could gradually evolve in the way described. Chance-plus-natural selection is plausible in a way that pure chance is not; but it is *not teleological*—i.e., it is a purely mechanistic or causal account of the formation of the structure, and thus has no need of postulated purposes of an intelligent creator. Hume seems to anticipate something like this Darwinian view in a remarkable passage in the *Dialogues:*

It is in vain, therefore, to insist upon the uses of the parts in animals or vegetables, and their curious adjustment to each other. I would fain know how an animal could subsist, unless its parts were so adjusted? Do we not find, that it immediately perishes whenever this adjustment ceases, and that its matter corrupting tries some new form? It happens, indeed, that the parts of the world are so well adjusted, that some regular form immediately lays claim to this corrupted matter: And if it were not so, could the world subsist? Must it not dissolve as well as the animal, and pass through new positions and situations; till in a great, but finite succession, it fall at last into the present or some such order? (Part VIII)

There is a very real sense, Hume seems to be saying, in which Paley and the other natural theologians of the world have the whole matter *exactly backwards*. They find it a near miracle that organs such as the eye should be so marvelously adapted for the organism's use, that the sexual organs should actually *fit* to make reproduction possible, and so on; thus they feel the need to postulate a supernatural intelligent creator to explain these miracles. But actually, on a Humean or Darwinian outlook, what we discover is *exactly what we should expect!* Organisms without a fine adaptation in their organs between structure and function simply would not have survived, and the true miracle would be to see organisms like that still around (unable to orient themselves in their environment, unable to fit their sexual organs in the right places for reproduction, but still here with lots of kids in spite of that)! Of course, we do not find such organisms; nature has weeded them out. Thus the eye, impressive as it is, is no miracle and no surprise, and thus we need nothing supernatural to account for it (even if we could make sense of whatever a supernatural account would be anyway).

So far, then, Hume has said this much: The universe is in some ways rather like a product of intelligent design (e.g., a watch) in that it has order and adaptation of structure to function. But there are many other objects (e.g., plants, animals, spider webs) that have comparable or even more impressive order and adaptation. But we seem perfectly able to explain these instances of order causally without postulating an intelligent designer. Thus order alone, even impressive order, does not give us strong grounds for inferring intelligent creation, much less supernatural creation. (Hume is, by the way, very suspicious of using a *part* of the world, whether a plant or a watch, as a basis of making guesses about the causes of the world itself. Who, he asks, has ever seen worlds in the making?)

Hume closes his attack on the design argument by making two final points: (1) The claims for order and design in the world are perhaps overblown. If the universe is like a watch, it is perhaps like a cheap watch. For there is plenty of evil and chaos in the world, and this certainly spoils the picture of perfect harmony and order that the defender of the design argument would like to have us see. (2) If the universe is really very, very like a humanly designed machine, then it seems to be the case that we are forced to conclude by analogy that the designer of the universe must be very, very like human designers. But what is true of human designers? Well, among other things, they grow old, die, fight with their wives, make mistakes, lie, and often work in committees or groups. So too, then, probably for God. This overly anthropomorphic view of God would be the outcome of the design argument if it really worked (if the analogy was really strong), and so, according to Hume, the devout and orthodox believer should actually be happy that it does not work. The conclusion that the believer wants (a single all-wise, all-good, and all-powerful Creator) is simply too strong given the available evidence.

So much, then, for the argument from design as developed and defended through the nineteenth century. Modern Scientific Creationists, though operating within the spirit of that argument, are now generally inclined to make a more modest claim—namely, that the evidence in support of the divine creation hypothesis is at least as strong as that in favor of the Darwinian evolutionary hypothesis. This means *either* that both are so evidentially weak as to be more religion than science and thus not properly taught in the public schools *or* that they are both scientific claims of equal credentials and should both be taught in public schools on an equal time basis. What is unacceptable given the evidence, according to the Scientific Creationists, is that Darwin should be taught as science and creationism should be left out as religion. (They never, so far as I can tell, face up to their most serious problem—namely, how can scientific sense or intelligibility be given to creation as supernatural causation?) Though the Hume-Natural Religion conflict sets the general stage for this contemporary conflict, the Scientific Creationists are specifically on the attack against Darwin and his followers. Thus it is to Darwin's theory that we shall now turn. Hume believed that he had shown that intelligent divine creation is not a reasonable scientific hypothesis; he also believed that he had shown that some mechanical causal process is at least as likely to be the explanation for order in the world as is the postulation of intelligent design. In vaguely anticipating the doctrine of natural selection, he even suggested what that process might be. Hume realized, however, that he was exploring the world of philosophical possibilities and ultimately concluded (Part VIII) that "a total suspense of judgment is here our only reasonable resource."

Put very simply, it was Darwin's great achievement to transform some of Hume's philosophical talk of "might be" into the scientific talk of "very probably is."[14] Darwin's account is a *theory*, of course, and there is always someone of smug ignorance who will seek to interpret the term "theory" as equivalent to "guess" or "specula-tion" as a way of discrediting the whole thing. But, of course, this is not what the concept of theory means in science. To call an account a theory is to say that it is an attempt to explain particular observations ("the facts") in terms of general or regular lawlike connections. The germ theory of disease is, in this sense, a theory, but, given all the evidence on its behalf, it is a *highly confirmed* theory and not mere guessing, speculaton, or myth making. Even the most ardent Scientific Creationist would not, I suspect, block having his child's life saved from scarlet fever by a penicillin injection by claiming that the germ theory of disease is "just a theory." He knows full well that this is a highly confirmed theory (in contrast to theories such as astrology, for example), and, if fair, he must take on the Darwinians by attempting to show, not that the Darwinian theory is just a theory, but rather that it is not a theory confirmed by the available evidence—that it is more like astrology than like the germ theory. The difficulty of such an attempt by the Creationist should come out from a discussion of Darwin's theory itself.

The Darwinian Revolution

As the foregoing discussion of Hume demonstrated, we did not need Darwin to discover problems for the teleological worldview of natural religion. Ample philosophical attacks against this view had already been mounted. Darwin was a scientist, not a philosopher, and thus his revolution was primarily a scientific one. His primary achievements as a scientist were two: (1) He helped confirm the claim that biological evolution (including human evolution) had in fact occurred. (2) He developed the principle of *natural selection* as the most probable theoretical explanation for that fact. We shall now explore each of these achievements in some detail.

EVOLUTION

Every great scientific theory is a response to some puzzle—some mystery which excites curiosity and wonder. A good theory will satisfy the curiosity and eliminate the mystery by letting us see in understandable ways how the thing that puzzled us was brought about. Thus we may legitimately ask just what puzzle or mystery so engaged Darwin that he began theorizing in response to it. Darwin answers this question himself at the very opening of his *The Origin of Species:*

When on board H. M. S. 'Beagle,' as naturalist, I was much struck with certain facts in the distribution of the inhabitants of South America, and in the geological relations of the present to the past inhabitants of that continent. These facts seemed to me to throw some light on the origin of species—that mystery of mysteries (Introduction p. 1)[15]

It is interesting to note that Darwin describes the origin of species as a *mystery*, thereby showing that he had clearly moved away in his thinking from the Genesis account of special creation. For one who subscribes to that account manifestly does not regard the origin of species as a mystery, but instead believes that he has the explanation for it—namely, God's work in the world, God's special creation of each species of plant and animal. But if species are not specially created by God, how can we explain their origin? The obvious alternative account, believed by many thinkers prior to Darwin's day, is in terms of *evolution*—descent with modification. We imagine some few primitive original forms and then imagine them gradually changing their forms and multiplying over countless generations until we have the rich and complex world that now presents itself to us—a world of millions of species (thousands of species of beetles alone).[16] This general idea has a long history,[17] so long indeed that we find the first expression of it in the pre-Socratic philosopher Anaximander (who "flourished" in 564 B.C.). Not only did Anaximander believe in evolution, but he also seemed to have some notion of survival of the fittest. Anaximander's views are reported by Theophrastus (371–286 B.C.) as follows:

Living creatures arose from the moist element as it was evaporated by the sun. Man was like another animal, namely, a fish, in the beginning. The first animals were produced in the moisture, each enclosed in a prickly bark. As they advanced in age, they came out upon the drier part. When the bark broke off, they survived for a short time. Further, he says that man was born from animals of another species. His reason is that while other animals quickly find food by themselves, man alone requires a lengthy period of suckling. Hence, had he been originally as he is now, he would never have survived. He declares that at first human beings arose in the inside of fishes, and after having been reared like sharks, and become capable of protecting themselves, they were finally cast ashore and took to land.[18]

We have already seen (in discussing Hume) that the rejection of supernatural special creation was not new with Darwin. Neither was the idea of evolution new with Darwin. What, then, was new with Darwin that makes his writing in this area so important—so important that we have now come to associate the concept of evolution with the name of Darwin? Very simply, it was this: Darwin was the first thinker to amass together, in one systematic volume ("one continuous argument" as he called it), *all* the evidence from various scientific fields of study relevant to this topic. The evidence, when brought together, *converged*[19] so as to render special creation as highly improbable and organic evolution as very nearly irresistible. The fact of organic evolution seemed to cry out from the page when all the data, previously scattered, were assembled and ordered in this monumental and systematic way. Thus, even if Darwin had never developed the concept of natural selection as an explanation for the process of evolution (how it actually works), he would still have an honorable place in the history of biology for having given evolution the status of a *fact*. What was his evidence? Drawn from various fields of scientific study, it consisted mainly of the following:

Variation Under Domestication. The first chapter of Darwin's *Origin of Species* is devoted to a discussion of the process of selective breeding, by human beings, of animals and plants. Darwin discusses such breeding because it represents proof, available for all to see, that species are capable of modification. Consider the many forms of domestic pigeons derived from one ancestor, or the many forms of dogs that have been derived from one or a few wolflike ancestors. Indian corn or maize is an example from the plant kingdom. Evolution would not be possible unless species were capable of modification; and the whole evolutionary story would not even be plausible unless it were possible to get multiple forms from one or a small number of distant ancestors. Studies of domestic breeding show that such modification and descent do occur.

Embryology. Darwin noted that the embryos of many different species (pig, dog, human, etc.) are remarkably similar in appearance and structure and that the ontogeny of an individual animal (its embryonic and later development) seems to pass through an evolutionary history, thereby providing evidence for common ancestry. He writes:

How, then, can we explain these several facts in embryology,—namely the very general, but not universal difference in structure between the embryo and the adult;—of parts in the same individual embryo, which ultimately become very unlike and serve for diverse purposes, being at this early period of growth alike;—of embryos of different species within the same class, generally, but not universally, resembling each other;—of the structure of the embryo not being closely related to its conditions of existence, except when the embryo becomes at any period of life active and has to provide for itself;—of the embryo apparently having sometimes a higher organisation than the mature animal, into which it is developed. I believe that all these facts can be explained . . . on the view of descent with modification (Chapter XIII, pp. 442–43).

Comparative Anatomy. Darwin called this "morphology" and it is one of the main sources of evidence for evolution. Comparisons of the forelimb skeletons of a frog, lizard, bird, cat, horse, and man show striking similarities difficult to explain except in terms of derivation, with modification, from a common ancestor.

Geology and the Fossil Record. The fossil record is much richer (particularly with respect to human evolution) than it was in Darwin's day. Darwin discusses the record available to him in Chapters IX and X of the *Origin.* The fossil record reveals many extinct species, some of which are sufficiently similar in morphology to present species so that it is plausible to think of them as distant ancestors. As Darwin recognized, the fossil record is sketchy and incomplete, and the evidence is not as strong as one would like. Still, he argued, what there is points in the direction of evolution. Darwin's reading of Lyell and other geologists, his own studies of the formation of coral reefs, and his observations of earthquakes in South America, all persuaded him that the earth's crust is not static, but is in perpetual flux and undergoing its own evolutionary descent with modification. Studies of rock strata provide evidence of past activity and show that the earth is of great age. The fossil record correlates with these observed strata (very roughly: the more primitive forms are found at lower and thus older strata), and thus the evidence of geological change and the evidence of biological change is mutually reinforcing. (How pleased Darwin would have been had he lived to see the technique of potassium/argon dating and to see how improved the fossil record now is. We now have, for example, the following "links" or intermediate forms: crossopterygian lobe-finned fishes with air-breathing lungs and walking fins appropriate for leaving water and going onto land; *Archaeopteryx* as a link between birds and reptile ancestors; and, most thrilling of all, forms linking modern man to his prehuman ancestors.[20])

Biogeography. Darwin claimed that what he observed in South America and the Galapagos was, to him, the most impressive evidence for evolution. He writes:

The most striking and important fact for us in regard to the inhabitants of islands, is their affinity to those of the nearest mainland, without being actually the same species. Numerous instances could be given of this fact. I will give only one, that of the Galapagos Archipelago, situated under the equator, between 500 and 600 miles from the shores of South America. Here almost every product of the land and water bears the unmistakeable stamp of the American continent. There are twenty-six land birds, and twenty-five of these are ranked . . . as distinct species, supposed to have been created here; yet the close affinity of most of these birds to American species in every character, in their habits, gestures, and tones of voice, was manifest. So it is with the other animals, and with nearly all the plants. . . . The naturalist, looking at the inhabitants of these volcanic islands in the Pacific, distant several hundred miles from the continent, yet feels that he is standing on American land. Why should this be so? Why should the species which are supposed to have been created in the Galapagos Archipelago, and nowhere else, bear so plain a stamp of affinity to those created in America? There is nothing in the conditions of life, in the geographical nature of the islands, in their height or climate, . . . which resembles closely the conditions of the South American coast: in fact there is considerable dissimilarity in all these respects. . . . I believe this grand fact can receive no sort of explanation on the ordinary view of independent creation; whereas on the view here maintained, it is obvious that the Galapagos Islands would be likely to receive colonists, whether by occasional means of transport or by formerly continuous land, from America; . . . and that such colonists would be liable to modification;—the principle of inheritance still betraying their original birthplace (Chapter XII, pp. 398–399).

This massive amount of data could, of course, be explained in any number of roundabout and *ad hoc* ways. But to a person having a clear mind unencumbered with any antecedent belief about the kind of explanation one would *like* to have and ready to respond to the most simple and elegant explanation of a complex phenomenon, then all the mass of data seem to converge on one inescapable fact: *evolution*, descent with modification. The many life forms (species) now present in the world are descended, with modification and over millions of generations, from some one or small set of original and primitive life forms. These life forms and the "links" or intermediate forms are all extinct, but the record of some of them (fewer than one would like, of course) is to be found in collected and observed fossils. The contemporary biologist, P. J. Darlington, Jr., writes as follows:

The clearest evidences of the fact of evolution, the evidences that first impressed Darwin and that anyone can see, are the geographic patterns made by evolving plants and animals on the earth's surface. The patterns can hardly be explained except as products of an ongoing evolution which gradually produces change and diversification among all living things everywhere. The fossil record is decisive too, but not so visible to most observers. And additional evidence comes from virtually every subfield of biology; modifications of domestic animals and plants under selection by man, and detailed homologies revealed by comparative anatomy are perhaps most easily appreciated. . . . Gaps and anomolies occur in the factual record, but are to be expected. . . . *Webster's Collegiate* defines proof as 'that degree of cogency, arising from evidence, which convinces the mind of any truth or fact and produces belief.' Different minds will require different 'degrees of cogency,' but I think that most persons who look at the evidence for themselves, and are not prevented by religious or political prejudices (i.e., by judgments before the evidence) will accept evolution as a fact.[21]

Almost all contemporary biologists accept evolution as a fact, although there is considerable disgreement among them concerning the *details* of evolution and its explanation. There is, however, no serious disagreement that the general structure of the Darwinian account is correct.[22]

The Scientific Creationists, of course, are always delighted to see any disagreement within the enemy camp, and they are invariably inclined to treat these disagreements as positive evidence for their own strange views. This is, of course, a mistake. Though there are disagreements about the *rate* of evolution (Is it always gradual as Darwin said or does it sometimes involve radical jumps to new species?) and about the *level* at which evolutionary processes work (Do they work at the micro level as Darwin suggested or is there significant macroevolution?), these disagreements take place *within* a framework that is fundamentally Darwinian. It is certainly a framework that is mechanistic and rejects any notion of teleology just as firmly as Darwin ever did.

Sometimes the Creationists' arguments are valuable simply for the comic relief they provide. Let me briefly consider just two of these:

The fossil record is to be explained, not by evolution, but by Noah's flood. Some early natural theologians explained the fossil record as a divine hoax—tricks placed in nature by God to test the strength of our faith. A more contemporary view is this: when the Great Flood came, the animals attempted to save themselves by scrambling to higher ground and (of course) the more primitive ones were slower and got stuck at lower geological levels. This accounts for the apparently progressive nature of the fossil record. Now this explanation is, of course, *logically possible*—i.e., its description is not self-contradictory. But can anything more positive be said in favor of it? Is there one single *reason* for believing it to be true? *Of course not!* (There is religious prejudice, but that is a cause for belief rather than a reason.) How incredible to imagine, for example, that not a single higher animal *tripped,* fell way down, and got drowned (and thus fossilized) at a lower level!

*The Second Law of Thermodynamics teaches that in any system random-
ness increases—a tendency from order to disorder—and thus the evolutionary claim that increased order and complexity arise progressively from
the more primitive is incompatible with physics.* This, of course, is a
simple-minded misunderstanding (or willful misstatement) of the
Second Law of Thermodynamics, one for which we would fail a
student in highschool physics. The Second Law of Thermodynamics applies only to *closed systems*—i.e., systems into which no new
usable energy is coming. If usable energy is coming into a system
(i.e., if the system is open), then order and complexity can arise
within that system—a subsystem of the whole. Since new usable
energy constantly comes into the earth from the sun, the earth is
not a closed system, and thus the Law is in no way incompatible
with the growth and complex development of life on earth.

But enough is enough! I am at the end of my patience and am
convinced that it is time to stop talking about this Scientific
Creationism nonsense. Thus I *will* stop talking about it, and I
advise others to do likewise. It is simply pseudo-science: a mixture
of claims that are too mysterious and obscure to have scientific
status (e.g., supernatural causation); claims that though scientifically intelligible, are too improbable to take seriously (e.g., animals
scrambling up the hills to escape the flood); gross misunderstand-
ings of other fields of science (e.g., misunderstanding of the
Second Law of Thermodynamics); and the ignorant or dishonest
misrepresentation of the implications of disagreements within the
community of reputable evolutionary biologists (e.g., suggesting
that if gradualism goes, teleology comes in). These people are quite
simply *cranks* and can be relegated to the company of astrologers,
alchemists, and members of the Flat Earth Society.

Let us, then, accept evolution as a fact—a process of descent
with modification that actually occurred in the plant and animal
kingdoms. At this point, of course, those of a theoretical cast of
mind (i.e., those interested not merely in facts, but in explanations
for those facts) will naturally ask *how* such evolution occurs—what
is the process or mechanism that tells us exactly how it happens
that the new and complex can emerge from the old and simple?
Darwin's single greatest contribution was in the answer he gave to
this question: the theory of *natural selection*.

NATURAL SELECTION.

The doctrine of natural selection is so striking in its simplicity that it can be stated briefly and clearly. Animals under domestication exhibit variations. Some forms can be encouraged and perpetuated and others extinguished by selective breeding; this is the mechanism of artificial selection. Could there be, Darwin asked, anything in nature operating analogously to a mechanism of artificial selection? His reading of Malthus persuaded him that there is.

Thomas Malthus was a political economist who in 1798 published his famous *An Essay on the Principle of Population.* The subject of this essay was the relationship between population and food supply.

The main contention was that, while population tends to increase by geometrical progression, food production, save in exceptional circumstances, can only be advanced by arithmetical progression. Consequently there is always a pressure of population on the means of subsistence, and the growth of population is kept down by a high death-rate due to poverty, disease, war, and vice. A great proportion of births are destined not to reach maturity. [23]

There is a struggle for existence (against nature, against other species, and against other members of one's own species) in an environment of scarce resources wherein not all will survive and reproduce. Only some will—the strongest and most adequately adapted (for getting food, avoiding predators, protecting eggs or young, etc.) The biological world, to use a phrase made famous by Herbert Spencer, operates on one simple principle: "survival of the fittest."

How could this Malthusian model give Darwin an analogue to artificial selection and explain the emergence of new species from old? The occurrence of variations within members of the same species was a known fact. Given all the possible variations, we can imagine that some will give the animals having them competitive advantage over those not having them (e.g., a slightly stronger beak might allow the animal to crack a certain kind of seed uncrackable by his fellows and thus expand his food supply). Those animals having such advantageous variations are more likely to survive and reproduce, and thus over many generations there will be an increase in the proportion of animals so advantaged and ultimately, perhaps, the extinction of the others. But this process can happen again (e.g., to the stronger beak is added a slightly different feather pattern making the bird somewhat more camouflaged and thus less vulnerable to preditors). This bird will also be more likely to survive and reproduce. When it does so survive and reproduce it will be said to have been *naturally selected*, with competition in an environment of scarce resources operating like an artificial breeder, a kind of "invisible hand" that makes a process appear purposive or teleological when it is actually quite mechanical.[24] Imagine enough such variations arising and being perpetuated through many generations by natural selection and you can easily imagine how eventually a creature could result sufficiently different from its original ancestor to constitute a new species. You can also easily imagine (as illustrated by Darwin's Galapagos finches) how many different species could have developed from a common ancestor. Indeed, no other explanation seems able to account for the striking similarity amid radical species diversity that the world actually exhibits. This is the theory of natural selection—simple, elegant, and powerful. To see its power at work, recall Paley's rhapsodic admiration for the human eye, a structure so wonderful and complex that only the miracle of special supernatural creation could account for it. Here is what Darwin has to say on this:

To suppose that the eye, with all its inimitable contrivances for adjusting the focus to different distances, for admitting different amounts of light, and for the correction of spherical and chromatic aberration, could have been formed by natural selection, seems, I freely confess, absurd in the highest possible degree. Yet reason tells me, that if numerous gradations from a perfect and complex eye to one very imperfect and simple, each grade being useful to its possessor, can be shown to exist; if farther, the eye does vary ever so slightly, and the variations be inherited, which is certainly the case; and if any variation or modification in the organ be ever useful to an animal under changing conditions of life, then the difficulty of believing that a perfect and complex eye could be formed by natural selection, though insuperable by our imagination, can hardly be considered real (Chapter VI, pp. 186–87).

The only real theoretical problem remaining for Darwin was this: how do the variations themselves arise and how are they perpetuated from generation to generation? Darwin generally expressed ignorance as to how variations arose, made some remarks about chance, or (in later editions of the *Origin*) even suggested that they might be "breathed in" by "the Creator." And on the problem of how they are passed from generation to generation, he sometimes expressed sympathy with Lamarck's notion of the inheritance of acquired characteristics. Basically, however, he was an honest man and admitted that he simply did not know. He had a great theory of the origin of species, but no clear theory on the origin and perpetuation of the variations upon which the origin of species depends.

As is generally well known, the Darwinian theory required completion by a theory of genetics and heredity. We now know that genes (units of DNA molecules) cause traits in the organism's physical structure. When DNA replicates it passes on the code for producing those same traits in succeeding generations. These genes can be caused to change in their molecular structure or arrangement (e.g., by radiation), and such changes are called *mutations*. When mutations occur, they will often cause physical variations in the organism or in the organism's progeny—some of them lethal or harmful, some of them neutral, and some of them beneficial or adaptive for the organism. A very big change could conceivably produce a new species instantly, but, more commonly, small variations over great spans of time gradually produce, through repeated workings of natural selection, new forms. It is this union of Darwinian theory and modern genetics that has come to be called the Modern Synthesis, or what might better be called Contemporary Darwinism. Since there is probably no field of biology where the rate of exciting discoveries is greater than in genetics, the simplistic picture I have given here cannot come close to doing justice to the actual complexities of the current state of the art. What form the Darwinian structure will ultimately take (even the extent to which it will remain truly Darwinian) will depend in large measure on discoveries in genetics and molecular biology. This is currently where the "action" is.[25]

The Descent of Man

Suppose that one accepts the general story of evolution by genetics plus natural selection. Where does *man* fit into all of this? In one of the great understatements in the history of thought, Darwin makes only one passing reference to human evolution in the *Origin*: "Much light will be thrown on man and his history." That is all. One could, of course, interpret this as Darwin being cautious and desiring to avoid, at least temporarily, the heated controversies that any discussion of human evolution would surely generate. But there is another possible interpretation—namely that, given all that had been said, human evolution follows as a matter of course. If we are persuaded by Darwin's general theory (and if we have no prior religious commitments) we would of course *expect* human beings to be a part of this evolutionary process and would be surprised if they were not. Certainly Darwin's critics realized this, for it is hard to imagine that clergymen such as Bishop Wilberforce would have cared about mere animal evolution if, like Descartes, they had believed that animals and humans are utterly dissimilar. He clearly saw what was coming, however, and (in his famous debate with "Darwin's Bulldog" Thomas Henry Huxley[26]) attacked Darwin for making a monkey out of man long before Darwin actually published his own thoughts on human evolution in *The Descent of Man* (1871). In this book, of course, the clergy's worst fears (and what should have been every reasonable person's expectations) were confirmed: Darwin did argue for the evolution of human beings (the species *homo sapiens*) from more primitive nonhuman (specifically sapian) forms. He did this initially by stressing physical similarities between man and other animals:

It is notorious that man is constructed on the same general type or model with the other mammals. All the bones in his skeleton can be compared with the corresponding bones in a monkey, bat, or seal. So it is with his muscles, nerves, blood-vessels, and internal viscera. The brain, the most important of all the organs, follows the same law (Chapter 1).

Darwin continually hammered home the point that the differences between humans and other animals are ones of degree, not of kind, and that the specifically human physical characteristics should be seen as having evolved (via natural selection) from other forms.

It is not physical similarity or evolution of physical forms that provokes the serious controversy, however. One might be happy to surrender the body up to Darwinism so long as the mind or spirit remains invulnerable to evolutionary explanation; for it is the realm of mind or spirit that seems most uniquely human and seems to represent a difference in kind, and not just degree, between human and nonhuman animals. Darwin sees this and faces it as the greatest challenge to his theory. Man's intellectual and moral qualities (especially the latter) are granted by Darwin to be the most essentially human features of man. If they can be brought into the orbit of evolutionary explanation, then the entire case for the descent of man is made; if they cannot be, then the theory must accept a major defeat. In Chapters III–V of *The Descent of Man*, Darwin makes his strongest case for an evolutionary explanation of the origin of these very special attributes. Is Darwin's case a success? This question is the topic of the next chapter.

Notes

1. This chapter is a very simplified overview of the Darwinian revolution, its background, and its implications. Since it contains simplifications, it also inevitably contains distortions, and I make no pretense that it contains a complete or totally accurate portrayal of the matters under discussion. Neither do I make any pretense that I am an expert in these matters. The chapter is offered as a kind of undergraduate level lecture on the issues and is presented here solely for those persons who really know little or nothing about Darwin's theory. Those who already have a good general knowledge on these matters are invited to skip the chapter entirely. Those who want a more expert and detailed treatment should have a look at some or all of the following (some of them being quite useful to me in composing the present chapter): Michael Ruse, *The Darwinian Revolution: Science Red in Tooth and Claw* (Chicago: University of Chicago Press, 1979) and his forthcoming *Darwinism Defended: A Guide to the Evolution Controversies*; Benjamin Farrington, *What Darwin Really Said* (New York: Schocken, 1966); P. J. Darlington, Jr., *Evolution for Naturalists* (New York: Wiley, 1980); Neal C. Gillespie, *Charles Darwin and the Problem of Creation* (Chicago: University of Chicago Press, 1979); and Dov Ospovat, *The Development of Darwin's Theory* (Cambridge: Cambridge University Press, 1981).

2. For example, see René Descartes, *Meditations on First Philosophy* (1641).

3. When I say that deterministic psychology is a "natural outgrowth" of Darwin's theory I mean to suggest that there is what Hume would have called a "tendency of the mind" to regard the former as in some sense proven by the latter. My own view, however, is that this tendency is logically misleading—i.e., that psychological determinism is *not* established by Darwin's theory. I discuss this in some detail in Chapter 3

where I distinguish between giving a biological explanation for the origin and preservation of a certain capacity (e.g., to think) and giving a biological explanation for a particular actual use of that capacity (e.g., deciding to stop smoking because I have been persuaded by the evidence that it is bad for my health). The fact that Darwin and others are able to give biological explanations of the first sort does not entail that biological explanations of the second sort are possible—a point sometimes missed by those who call themselves "biological determinists."

4. See Chapter 1, Note 3.

5. My first-hand knowledge of contemporary Scientific Creationism is based on one book: H. M. Morris, editor, *Scientific Creationism* (San Diego: Creation-Life Press, 1974).

6. In the old days (e.g., in the days of the famous Scopes trial), the teaching of evolution was opposed on grounds that were openly religious in nature. As one will quickly discover from reading the recent Arkansas case in Appendix A to this book, contemporary Creationists are more subtle. They appeal to our liberal sentiments of fair play by arguing that the empirical evidence alone does not allow us to chose between Darwinism and Creationism, and thus, in fairness, both should be treated equally (either not taught at all or both given equal emphasis).

7. For Hume's views on causation, see *Treatise*, Book I, Part III, Sections I-VIII, XI-XII, XIV-XV, and *Enquiry Concerning Human Understanding*, Sections IV-VIII.

8. Another kind of miracle claim would, of course, cause more problems for Hume—namely, *contemporary* reports of events observed under controlled conditions (e.g. under examination of scientists and professional magicians). For Hume's views on the causal origin of religious beliefs generally, see his *The Natural History of Religion* (1777).

9. William Paley, *Natural Theology, or Evidences of the Existence and Attributes of the Deity Collected from the Appearances of Nature* (1802). This book was widely taught in English universities in the nineteenth century, and Darwin knew it well.

10. In developing my discussion of analogical arguments, I have drawn heavily on the excellent treatment provided by the late James Cornman in Chapter Five of *Philosophical Problems and Arguments* by James W. Cornman and Keith Lehrer, Second Edition (New York: Macmillan, 1974). James Cornman was one of my teachers whom I respected and admired, and I believe that his early death by accident was a great loss to contemporary philosophy.

11. *Supra* note 10, p. 373.

12. It would, of course, beg the very question at issue if one said that, since these are all God's creatures, there is a background teleology at work.

13. By the term "chance" here all I mean is "unpredictable," not "uncaused." As we now know from genetics (see discussion below), these variations may be caused by mutations. They are still unpredictable with respect to particular cases, however, and can only be discussed statisti-

cally (unless, of course we *make* them come about through genetic engineering). Of course, even purely chance mechanisms can produce order—e.g., normal curves.

14. I do not mean at all to suggest that, as a matter of historical fact, Darwin was influenced by Hume's *Dialogues*. Indeed, the available evidence suggests that he was not. As an expository or pedagogical device, however, I think it is valuable to use Hume in order to "set up" a logical and epistemological framework in which Darwin's ideas can be viewed from a philosophical perspective.

15. *On the Origin of Species by Means of Natural Selection, or The Preservation of Favoured Races in the Struggle for Life*, First Edition, 1859. All page references are to the facsimile edition published by Harvard University Press in 1964.

16. Beetles have an interesting if minor role in the history of the development of evolutionary theory. Darwin was very fond of collecting them, and Thomas Henry Huxley, attempting to ridicule the implausibility of the Creationist claim, noted the large number of species and wryly remarked that "God must have had an inordinate fondness for beetles."

17. See the article "Evolutionism" by Thomas A. Goudge in Volume II of the *Dictionary of the History of Ideas*, ed. Philip Wiener (New York: Scribners, 1973).

18. Quoted in John Burnet, *Early Greek Philosophy*, Fourth Edition (London: Macmillan, 1930) pp. 70–71.

19. The English philosopher of science William Whewell (1794–1866) spoke of a "convergence of inductions" when empirical evidence from various sources all pointed to the same result.

20. See P. J. Darlington, Jr., *supra* note 1.

21. *Ibid.*, pp. 32–33.

22. Two major contemporary disagreements concern the *rate* of evolutionary change and the *level* at which that change occurs. These are related. According to Darwin, the evolutionary process is gradual because it involves natural selection working over time to favor those individuals having small advantaging variations. It thus takes a very long time to get a new species. Recently, however, the theory of *punctuated equilibrium* has been articulated as an account which accords better with the gaps found in the fossil record. According to this theory, much evolutionary change is gradual and stable. Sometimes, however, because perhaps of large-scale genetic events, there will be a sudden "jump" to a new species without an intermediate form. Thus, instead of variations being selected, new individuals will be selected–macroevolution instead of microevolution. All of this is explained very clearly in Steven M. Stanley's *The New Evolutionary Timetable* (New York: Basic Books, 1981). As Stanely realizes, this new theory is not the wholesale abandonment of Darwin and should provide no comfort to Scientific Creationists. These debates within the field of evolutionary biology are raising the *real* intellectual excitement, and it would be a shame if our attention is diverted from them by silly worries about Scientific Creationism.

23. Farrington, *supra* note 1, p. 46.

24. The Scottish economic theorist Adam Smith (1723–1790) used the metaphor of the "invisible hand" in his influential *An Inquiry Into the Nature and Causes of the Wealth of Nations* in his account of how laissez-faire capitalism (in his judgment) allowed community good to come about, as if by an invisible hand, from the private pursuit of individual self-interest. Darwin was, of course, familiar with this book.

25. For a readable (but no doubt already outdated) account of contemporary molecular biology and genetics, see Horace Freeland Judson's *The Eighth Day of Creation: The Makers of the Revolution in Biology* (New York: Simon and Schuster, 1979).

26. For an account of this debate, see pp. 242 ff. of Ruse's *The Darwinian Revolution, supra* note 1.

3

Darwin and the Origin of Morality

> If we answered love with hate, or came to dislike those who acted fairly toward us, or were averse to activities that furthered our good, a community would soon dissolve. Beings with a different psychology either have never existed or must soon have disappeared in the course of evolution.
>
> JOHN RAWLS, *A Theory of Justice*

There are at least three related but different ways in which one could attempt to bring the facts and theories of evolutionary biology to bear on moral phenomena: (1) One could attempt to derive or rationally prove substantive moral principles from the facts of evolution; (2) one could attempt to explain the causal origin of certain moral principles (e.g., altruism); or (3) one could attempt to explain moral psychology, the causal origin of *conscience* (i.e., the capacity to be motivated by moral considerations).

The notion of "evolutionary ethics" tends to have bad press among professional moral philosophers because the phrase generally calls to mind only the first attempt mentioned above—i.e., the attempt to derive substantive moral principles from the facts of biology. The mistakes of such an attempt are well-known and obvious; so well-known and obvious that one of them has even been given a name: the naturalistic fallacy. As has been pointed out by philosophers from Hume to G. E. Moore, one cannot logically derive a statement about what ought to be the case from any statement of what simply is, in fact, the case. Thus, because it might be the case that in nature the physically stronger survive, it cannot follow from this, in any moral or ethical sense, that they ought to survive or that their survival is morally good. It is logically possible (not to mention empirically common) to be indifferent to the future welfare of the human species, to those future "possible people" who will populate the earth after we are gone. (Hume puts the point this way: " 'Tis not contrary to reason to prefer the destruction of the whole world to the scratching of my little finger."[1]) And if one can consistently be indifferent to *that*, then *a fortiori* one can consistently be indifferent to any moral principle that one might attempt to pluck from evolutionary theory.[2]

Thus, no matter how fancy and modern the "scientific" dress they may wear, biological attempts to derive what is moral from what is biologically the case are just as problematic as the intellectually bankrupt tradition of Natural Law (in Catholic moral theology) which they formally resemble—much to the dismay and embarrassment of all parties concerned, no doubt. Recall a characteristic Natural Law move: "Oral copulation is morally evil because it is contrary to nature (or a crime against nature)." What in the world, or out of it, could this possibly mean? One meaning of "contrary to nature" is this: an event is contrary to nature if, given the laws of nature, it could not happen, its occurrence is causally impossible. This is, of course, a definition of a *miracle*, and I doubt that anyone really ever meant to suggest that oral copulation is miraculous or immoral on that account. Besides, if this sexual activity were contrary to nature in this sense, it would not (because could not) occur, and thus there would be nothing to worry about. Another meaning of "contrary to nature" is perhaps this: an event is contrary to nature if it is improbable, i.e., if its occurrence is statistically infrequent. But this surely cannot be a moral criterion for it would condemn as immoral such unusual but quite valuable things as heroism and genius. What then does "contrary to nature" mean? Ultimately, I suspect, the claim that something is contrary to nature is—in Catholic moral theology—simply an obscurantist way of saying that God does not approve of it, that it is not consistent with the plans or purposes in terms of which He created human beings, placed them in nature, and thereby provided meaning for their lives. But, for all the reasons noted in the first chapter, this, even if true, could not provide a rational foundation for moral principles or for meaning *in* human life. The upshot, then, is this: Catholic moral theologians, evolutionary ethicists, and hippie flowerchildren to the contrary, the "naturalness" of something, whether sexual conduct or herb teas, is not necessarily a morally recommending feature of that thing; nor is the "unnaturalness" of something necessarily a condemning feature of it.[3] These evaluative matters would have to be decided, if they are decidable, on the basis of other criteria. The facts of evolutionary biology might, when conjoined with a principle that " 'ought' implies 'can' ", *rule out* certain moral principles as inconsistent with human nature. Biology can perhaps do this negative job.[4] Also, *given* certain moral principles about how human beings should be treated, the facts of evolutionary biology might force us to expand the range of those principles by teaching us that there is greater continuity in morally relevant respects between human and other animals than we might initially have supposed. In this way evolutionary biology can be an aid to substantive moral thought. What it cannot be, however, is an independent *source* of positive moral principles. If it attempts to play this role, it is in no better shape, in spite of its scientific pretensions, than those religious and philosophical attempts to derive morality and meaning that were considered and rejected in the first chapter.

Now it is interesting, and much to his credit, that Darwin makes no attempt to derive substantive moral principles from biological phenomena, and thus, to the extent that he is engaged in something which might be called "evolutionary ethics," his work is generally free of the simple-minded mistakes just noted. His discussion of morality in *The Descent of Man* (Chaps. III, IV, V, and XXI especially) abounds with substantive moral principles, but they are simply assumed by Darwin as part of the conventional moral outlook of his day. He expresses allegiance to some unclear combination of utilitarianism, Kantianism, and the Golden Rule, but he makes no attempt to derive or rationally prove these from the facts of biology. (If Darwin is a moral conservative, it is not because his biology makes him one.) At most he attempts to show that his favored set of moral principles is consistent with the known facts of human biology in a way that other principles (e.g., extreme anti-altruism) would not be, and thus he makes the negative point that our conventional morality is, at least, not to be condemned as impossible or unrealistic. Beyond this he does not go.

But if Darwin is not concerned to derive or rationally prove substantive moral principles, what then is he up to in those three long chapters in *The Descent of Man* devoted to morality and the moral sense? What he says is that he wants to view morality "exclusively from the side of natural history," and by this he clearly means an inquiry into the causal origins of morality, both of certain moral principles and the moral sense or conscience. It is his causal account of origins which will be evolutionary in nature and which will employ the notion of natural selection. The idea of "survival of the fittest" will explain the origin of moral principles and conscience; it will *not* be offered as itself a substantive moral principle, nor will it be put forth as a principle from which substantive moral principles may be derived.

We turn, then, to the question of origins, and I can anticipate a concern from certain quarters about the legitimacy of a philosopher troubling himself with such matters. (Recall my discussion of the genetic fallacy in Chapter 1.) Much of the important pre-Kantian moral philosophy (e.g., that of David Hume) regarded the question of causal origins as central to its enterprise. Since Kant, however, it has been common to accept the following dichotomy: Inquiries into causal origins are empirical and are thus the business of science; *a priori* or conceptual inquiries are the business of philosophy. I would like here to explore the matter in some detail in order to justify my conviction that philosophy is ill-served (and even borders on the inane) if it operates on too narrow a conception of what constitutes its business.[5]

Why, then, should the moral philosopher care about theories of moral origins? Why should he care about the causal production of moral principles or of conscience? There are, I think, two important reasons why he should so care.

First, it is important to realize that many theories that, on the surface, seem purely empirical and scientific actually contain or presuppose controversial conceptual components. The philosopher, who is supposedly good at sorting out conceptual puzzles, will perhaps be able to aid the empirical scientist in developing causal theories which are free of conceptual shortcomings. Unless he takes some shortsighted pleasure in seeing scientists make asses of themselves, the philosopher should surely regard such an activity as a worthwhile use of his professional time and energies. Let me give an example to illustrate the kind of point I am making: Freud's theory of moral psychology and development. Freud's theory on the surface seems purely empirical and causal: morality functions as a set of internal inhibitions whereby dangerous antisocial impulses are to be restrained or sublimated in order that culture may survive. These inhibitions are acquired in early childhood when the child, fearing among other things the withdrawal of love, internalizes the values of the father. These internalized values constitute his superego or conscience, and they, as Freud puts it, "retain the character of the father" who is the conduit whereby society's values are transmitted to the child. To put it briefly, the internal commands of conscience are the internal*ized* commands of the father. This is the origin of morality.

But is it? An analysis of the origin of morality will be correct only to the extent that it operates with a correct analysis of the concept of morality itself. But is it reasonable to regard morality as nothing but a set of internalized parental commands? Surely not. Part of the moral beliefs of any mature adult will, of course, be in some sense shadowy remnants of childhood commands. But we would regard as a moral imbecile—a moral child, actually—someone whose moral outlook consisted *solely* of such imitative responses. It is part of our concept of a morally mature person that such a person questions some accepted prohibitions, uses his reason to inquire into justifications for them, and retains them only if can see for himself that they have merit. This is what we think of as the minimal concept of a morally mature person. For most actual human beings, their morality will consist of some uncritically accepted commands (derived from parents and culture) and some critically thoughtout beliefs they have arrived at (or at least decided to keep) on their own by a process of critical, rational reflection. Freud's theory may be the correct causal account for the origin of the former, but it is worthless as an account of the latter. Thus if anyone claimed that Freud had a correct causal account of morality, that person would be wrong. Freud could not have a correct causal account of morality, for he has insufficient appreciation of the complex nature of the concept of morality itself. At most he has a correct causal account of part of morality. Freud's causal theory thus contains a philosophical flaw, and it is not surprising that his theory has now been supplemented within psychology by the theories of such philosophically sensitive writers as Piaget and Kohlberg who are concerned to stress that moral development is in part cognitive development.

Moving to sociobiology, we might, as philosophers, be on the lookout for similar flaws in these theories. For example, in much of the literature of sociobiology there is a tendency to equate morality with altruism, and sociobiological theories of the origin of morality are often theories of the origin of altruism. But if morality involves more than altruism, or if sociobiology has a defective concept of altruism itself, then to that degree the empirical and causal theory will be deficient. I shall say more about this in the final chapter, but I mention it now in order to alert you to the kind of objections a philosopher might legitimately make to what is put forth as a scientific or empirical theory.

It is, of course, fairly easy for philosophers to admit the relevance of science where this relevance consists simply of our smugly pointing out the conceptual mistakes scientists make. The second point I want to make about the relation between moral philosophy and empirical behavioral science, however, involves something much less to the liking of most philosophers—namely, my belief that philosophers have important things to learn from scientists, that their philosophical theories can be improved (or undermined) by scientific knowledge. The reason for this is simple: just as scientific theories can be defective because they uncritically presuppose a faulty philosophical or conceptual component, so can philosophical theories be defective if they presuppose a false or unreasonable scientific or empirical component.

Let me give a simple example to illustrate this. One of the most prominent theories of punishment within legal philosophy is the deterrence theory—i.e., the claim that punishment is justified by deterring potential criminals from illegal conduct. But what if psychologists discover that many or most criminals do not in fact calculate—i.e., rationally weigh alternatives—before engaging in criminal conduct? Surely this would render most of deterrence theory beside the point.

More germane to our present purposes is the way in which biological theories concerning the origin of morality and conscience could undermine moral theories. Let us take Kant's moral theory for an example. Darwin seems to admire Kant and even occasionally quotes his writings in moral philosophy with some understanding. For he sees in Kant a generally correct account of the concept of conscience or the moral sense—i.e., as a motive to do one's duty because one perceives that it is one's duty. After this initial agreement, however, Kant and Darwin part ways radically. For Kant, moral behavior (autonomous moral choice) is *rationally motivated* behavior, and, as such, it is not susceptible to causal or scientific explanation. (In Kant's language, it represents the *noumenal* aspect of the person; whereas only the *phenomenal* aspect of a person is open to causal explanation.) Thus Kant takes great (and often obscure) pains to argue that moral motivation, unlike all other motivation, is not a matter of acting to satisfy any *desire*.[6] Kant calls action motivated by the attempt to satisfy desire *heteronomous* and bans it from the moral realm. (He thus regards acts motivated by sympathy or kindness, or performed out of habit, as without moral worth.) Darwin, of course, disagrees, the whole point of the chapters on morality and moral motivation being, after all, to show its causal origins, how natural it is, how, in Kantian language, heteronomous it is. Darwin will not deny the importance of reason in the moral life of human beings, but he follows Hume in regarding reason as primarily a problem-solving capacity—an *instrument* that allows us to determine the most effective means for attaining the ends set by our passions or desire. He most certainly does *not* follow Kant in regarding reason as setting ends, as having the capacity to motivate independently of desire, or as being a noumenal faculty lying beyond the power of empirical science to explain.

Now it is important to see that this is not a matter on which Kant and Darwin could simply agree to disagree. It is not as though both had the same concept of morality and simply differed about its origins—like two persons agreeing on what symptoms constitute a certain disease, but disagreeing on its origin, one thinking it viral and the other thinking it bacterial. For Kant's very *conception of morality* involves the belief that moral motivation is not natural or causal in any ordinary sense. It is because we are autonomous self-legislators in the noumenal realm of reason that we are morally *special* creatures, and it is because we are special creatures that special moral requirements apply to us (e.g., always treat human beings as ends in themselves, and never as means only). Undermine our contra-causal moral autonomy and you undermine what is morally special about us; undermine what is morally special about us and you undermine the profound moral requirements that Kant builds into his categorical imperative. Kant would thus be most upset by any attempt to show that the human capacity for moral choice is simply a natural outgrowth, explained by the biological mechanism of natural selection, from a kind of rudamentary morality found in "the brutes," for this would show that human moral capacities differ only in degree and not in kind from those found in nonhuman animals.

There are, of course, two reasons why this Kantian anxiety attack might be premature: (1) the Darwinian account might not be true, or it might be incomplete and thus only partially true, and (2) the moral implications of the Darwinian account, even if true, might not be as grave as a rigid Kantian might suppose. Let me explore this latter point first.

"Moral requirements rest upon what is special or unique about human beings—what distinguishes them from other animals." This is a frequently repeated claim about morality (and not just by Kantians), but is it really correct? Does it really tell us very much? I think it is true only of the human species that many of its members urinate in urinals; and I have been told (probably at various cocktail parties) that human beings are the only animals who kill for sport, the only animals always in heat, the only animals to kiss on the mouth during sexual intercourse, and the only animals conscious of their own deaths. I do not know which if any of these observations is true; but let us suppose that all are. This would establish several ways in which human beings are unique—i.e., differ from other animals. But would anyone in his right mind attempt to build a moral theory on a basis so inane? Would anyone say with a straight face that human beings ought to be given special moral respect because they alone have the unique property of, for example, being always in heat? Surely not. The supposedly unique qualities that are actually chosen by moral philosophers are qualities like these: immortal soul, free will, autonomous rationality, etc. But these are valued, not because they are unique, but because of other evaluative considerations. They are considered ways in which human beings are *essentially* unique (kissing a sexual partner on the mouth being an *accidental* uniqueness), but the concept of *essentiality* here rests upon some independent moral evaluation; and thus it is difficult indeed to see how the essentiality could be the basis or foundation for morality and moral evaluation.

Let us ignore these skeptical doubts for a moment, however, and simply grant for purposes of discussion that human beings do uniquely possess certain morally relevant properties. Why would these become less important or less moral by virtue of being natural rather than transcendent or supernatural? I happen to agree with Kant that the capacity for moral choice is a very impressive attribute to find in a creature; but I fail to see why I should be more impressed by this capacity if I think that it is present because of some spooky metaphysical "Zap!" than because of some biological causal process. If anything I would be inclined to be more impressed by the latter because it at least renders the capacity intelligible and links it up to the natural world I understand and in which I live. Thus even if Kant was wrong in thinking that moral choice is *noumenally* special, he may still have been correct in thinking it *special* and in attempting to found moral principles upon it. And surely evolutionary thinking does not challenge specialness in every sense. After all, Darwin's theory is about *origins*—how the new emerges from the old. This is what makes it *evolution!* Therefore the Darwinian account, even if completely true, should be viewed more as an attempt to undermine certain metaphysical theories about morality than as an attempt to undermine morality itself. It will do the latter only if Kant's worst fears are well-founded—i.e., only if morality does indeed depend upon a certain metaphysical foundation. This is a very large issue, of course, but I have tried to sketch a couple of reasons for thinking that the Kantain fears might be a bit premature.[7]

But is the Darwinian account true? In order to consider this question we must examine the actual details of the theory itself. It is to this task that I shall now turn.

Darwin opens Chapter IV ("The Moral Sense") of *The Descent of Man* with these striking words:

I fully subscribe to the judgment of those writers who maintain that of all the differences between man and the lower animals, the moral sense or conscience is by far the most important. . . . It is summed up in that short but imperious word *ought,* so full of high significance. It is the most noble of all the attributes of man, leading him without a moment's hesitation to risk his life for that of a fellow-creature; or after due deliberation, impelled simply by the deep feeling of right or duty, to sacrifice it in some great cause (Chap. IV, p. 471).[8]

After informing the reader that he intends to treat the issue of morality "exclusively from the side of natural history," he then makes the following crucial remark:

The following proposition seems to me in a high degree probable— namely, that any animal whatever, endowed with well-marked social instincts, the parental and filial instincts being here included, would inevitably acquire a moral sense or conscience, as soon as its intellectual powers had become as well, or nearly as well developed, as in man (Chap. IV, p. 472).

Two important points emerge from these quoted remarks: (1) Darwin agrees with Kant that the moral sense or conscience is the most special feature of human beings. (The passage I quoted is immediately followed by Darwin quoting a particularly purple piece of Kantian prose in praise of the moral sense that begins: "Duty! Wonderous thought!") (2) Darwin's actual analysis of the *concept* of moral sense or conscience is remarkably Kantian in spirit. For notice his thought carefully: *If* an animal has social instincts, and *if* that animal is intelligent, *then* it will develop a moral sense. Darwin is not, as one might expect (or even conclude from a superficial reading), identifying social instincts with a moral sense. The mere instinctual desire to aid a fellow member of one's species, though part of the basis from which the moral sense must be built, is not itself the moral sense. These instincts or sentiments, of which sympathy is the most prominent, are morally important, but they by no means exhaust the crucial elements of moral psychology.

What, then, according to Darwin, must be added to sympathy in order to generate a true moral sense? In order to understand his account, let me introduce a distinction between what I shall call *primary desires* and *secondary desires* (or feelings, or impulses, or wants, or instincts). A primary desire is a desire to bring about a certain state of affairs in the external world—e.g., the gain of power, the assistance of someone loved, etc. A secondary desire is a *desire about a desire*—i.è., a desire to have certain desires or, more germane to our purposes, a desire to act out of one sort of desire rather than another. According to Darwin (as expounded in my language), the moral sense or conscience is the secondary desire to act out of certain primary desires, particularly those of sociability and sympathy that have the well-being of others as their object. Thus the relation of Darwin's account to that of Kant is actually more complicated than I suggested initially. Like Kant, Darwin realizes that there is something odd about identifying moral motivation simply with sympathy or benevolence (though Darwin would not rule them out of the moral realm entirely). The desire to do one's duty is simply not a desire of the same sort as the desire, for example, to help someone. The latter is a primary desire; the former is a secondary desire.

To see this, let us consider the nature of *moral failure* and how, according to Darwin, it differs from other sorts of failure to satisfy desire. If I have two primary desires that are incompatible, then I can at most satisfy one of them—e.g., I cannot both play tennis and read a novel at the same time. Let us suppose that I read the novel and do not play tennis. I may be disappointed about the lost tennis and sorry that I could not do both. I will not, however, have *self-critical* feelings about my failure to play tennis and think: "How *could* I be the sort of person who would give in to the desire to read instead of play tennis? Oh, how I hate myself! I *will* do better next time!" But exactly such feelings of self-condemnation are what we would expect where the unfulfilled desire has been moral in nature; and, if they did happen to be present in the tennis case, this would simply show that I had a moralistic attitude toward the playing of tennis. Darwin makes a self-critical attitude toward failure a part of his definition of conscience and writes as follows:

At the moment of action, man will no doubt be apt to follow the stronger impulse; and though this may occasionally prompt him to the noblest deeds, it will more commonly lead him to gratify his own desires at the expense of other men. But after their gratification, when past and weaker impressions are judged by the ever-enduring social instinct, and by his deep regard for the good opinion of his fellows, retribution will surely come. He will then feel remorse, repentance, regret, or shame. . . . He will consequently resolve more or less firmly to act differently for the future; and this is conscience; for conscience looks backwards, and serves as a guide for the future (Chap. IV, p. 484).

Darwin, analogously to both Kant and Freud, thus thinks of the moral sense as an "internal monitor" or "capacity for self-command" where this is understood to mean a capacity to be motivated to do something because of the belief that one ought to do so, the capacity to be self-critical when one fails so to be motivated, and the capacity to improve future behavior on the basis of such self-criticism. Unlike Kant, however, Darwin conceives of this conflict as entirely natural and sees it as a conflict between two empirical or psychological desires (desires of different kinds, yes, but still desires) and not between the natural realm of desire, on the one hand, and the (non-natural? supernatural? transcendent?) realm of the noumenal self on the other.

Darwin thus sets out to answer two empirical questions: (1) What is the origin of sympathy and other social instincts in human beings? Do we have these as a result of special implantation or creation of some kind, or can they be shown to have evolved by a process of natural selection? (2) What is the origin of those secondary desires that have the primary social desires as their object— i.e., why are the desires of sympathy reinforced and strengthened by the desire that one be motivated by them and the bad feelings (guilt, shame, etc.) that follow when one is not motivated by them? This is, of course, an inquiry into the moral sense or conscience.

First the social desires. Darwin's account of the evolutionary origin of human sociability is quite simple and may be summarized as follows: As animals, human beings are individually quite vulnerable. The survival of human beings, therefore, requires community life, for only in stable, cohesive groups can people flourish and compete with nature and other animals in the struggle for existence. The stability of primitive groups could not have been guaranteed by the artifices of advanced civilizations (e.g., legal systems, elaborate arguments from rational prudence, etc.) since the maintenance of such artifices would have required more sophistication than would have been possible for such peoples. Thus the stability had to be guaranteed by *affective* bonds between members of communities—i.e., bonds of feeling. In the struggle for survival, a community of human egoists would have been a suicide club. Darwin puts it this way:

With those animals which were benefited by living in close association, the individuals which took the greatest pleasure in society would best escape various dangers, whilst those that cared least for their comrades, and lived solitary, would perish in greater numbers. . . . In however complex a manner [sympathy] may have originated, as [the feeling] is one of high importance to all those animals which aid and defend one another, it will have been increased through natural selection; for those communities, which included the greatest number of the most sympathetic members, would flourish best, and rear the greatest number of offspring. . . . In order that primeval men, or the ape-like progenitors of man, should become social, they must have acquired the same instinctive feelings, which impel other animals to live in a body; and they no doubt exhibited the same general disposition. They would have felt uneasy when separated from their comrades, for whom they would have felt some degree of love; they would have warned each other of danger, and have given mutual aid in attack or defense. All this implies some degree of sympathy, fidelity, and courage. . . . Selfish and contentious people will not cohere, and without coherence nothing can be effected (Chaps. IV and V, pp. 478, 479 and 498).

The survival of human beings required that people *care* for each other in ways that, if not exactly moral, at least form the basis for moral caring. Care only for self, or even care limited to one's immediate family, would not have been sufficient. Survival required a more generalized caring for all members of one's community and, as the communities became more complex, for the rules establishing duties within the communities. Advanced or civilized morality, then, is not the artificial creation, *ex nihilo,* of something totally new. It is, rather, simply an increasingly disinterested and abstracted generalization of the primitive caring that insured the survival of human beings.

This, of course, is not all of Darwin's story. One could grant that social instincts allowed humans to survive and flourish, but still insist that these instincts are something unique and were implanted in early humans (Adam perhaps) by special creation and they are not the result of man's in any sense descending from other animals. In order to make the point he wants about origins, namely, that moral qualities are very probably the result of evolutionary descent, Darwin must attempt to establish a strong continuity between the human moral world and the moral world of other animals. (It would beg the question, of course, to deny that the word 'moral' can in any legitimate sense be applied to other animals.) Thus Darwin spends a great deal of space describing in a very anecdotal and entertaining way (especially for dog lovers) the social and intellectual qualities found in many higher animals, which are so striking in their similarity to those found in humans that only prejudice would prevent one from at least strongly considering the possibility of descent here. By showing that many human moral and intellectual qualities differ only in degree and not in kind from those present in other animals, and by explaining how natural selection would have favored the survival of those creatures in whom those qualities were highly developed, Darwin does not prove the evolutionary descent of human beings. But he certainly does make a major step in overcoming one large obstacle in the way of accepting that theory.

Having explored Darwin's account of the origins of the instincts of sociability, particularly sympathy, in human beings, we are now in a position to examine the other crucial component of his theory: the origin of the moral sense or conscience.

You will recall that Darwin regards conscience as an internal monitor: reinforcing the social instincts, occasioning self-condemnation in cases of moral failure, and prompting resolves for future moral improvement. Darwin sees this as involving, not a conflict between reason and the passions, but between two different sorts of passion—what I have called primary and secondary desires. Santayana once said that the essential dignity of man consisted in his ability to despise himself. Darwin might have disagreed that self-despisal is confined to the human species, but he surely would have agreed that an essential element of moral conscience is to be found in the realm of self-condemning feelings: regret, shame, guilt, remorse, and repentance.

What is the origin of these secondary, self-reflective feelings? Society, as Hume long before had pointed out, could not hold itself together and flourish (especially in times when the conflict between humans and other species must have been far greater than it is now) if each person reflected upon the intrinsic merits of each act before performing it. There must, therefore, be an unchallenged and unreflective acceptance of certain rules of conduct. These rules would not work, however, if their obedience depended upon a constant external threat—e.g., a policeman at every shoulder. Thus internal controls or monitors are required. These monitors are in the realm of feeling—strong feelings inclining us toward socially approved conduct, and strong feelings of self-condemnation if we fail to act in the proper way. These internal feelings insure that antisocial behavior (even if externally undetected) is never cost free—never without at least an internal price. And paying this internal price will, according to Darwin, incline us to do better next time.

Is Darwin then saying that the motivation of all behavior, even moral behavior, is selfish? No. In a passage reminiscent of Bishop Butler's writings against psychological egoism, Darwin notes that a selfish desire is a desire to benefit oneself. A moral desire is a desire to benefit the group. If I have such a moral desire it is, of course, *my* desire. This is a truth of grammar—all my desires being mine and, therefore, owned by me. Thus everytime I act I am, in a sense, doing something I want to do; since of necessity I am acting to satisfy one of my own wants or desires. But is this selfishness? Surely not; for the desire of mine must be more than mine in order to be selfish; it must also have my own welfare as its object, as the state of affairs I seek to bring about. Suppose I go to my wife and say this: "I love you more than anything in the world. All I care about is making you happy, and all I want to do is act for your benefit." How strange if she replied: "Selfish bastard! There you go again caring only about yourself, satisfying your own wants." Darwin writes as follows:

Thus the reproach is removed [that we lay] the foundation of the noblest part of our nature in the base principle of selfishness; unless, indeed, the satisfaction which every animal feels, when it follows its proper instincts, and the dissatisfaction felt when prevented, be called selfish (Chap. IV, p. 490).

Kant, in addition to his worries about determinism, refused to locate moral motivation in the realm of desire because he was strongly tempted to subscribe to some simple version of psychological egoism—i.e. to believe that if a person acts to satisfy one of his own desires, then that person is acting selfishly. Seeing clearly that morality is not a matter of mere selfishness, Kant thus had an extra reason for removing it from the realm of desire entirely. Not so with Darwin who clearly sees that many morally relevant desires are not (in any useful or ordinary sense) selfish or egoistic. Indeed one desire that plays a large role in Darwin's account of the origin of the moral sense is a crucial element of sympathy: the innate desire for approval of others. The desire to be approved by one's fellows is, according to Darwin, a primary reinforcer of moral rules, at least those that involve social benefit. And surely he is at least partially correct here—something we can see by considering the concept of *shame*, one of those crucial self-condemning feelings that in part make up the internal monitor of conscience. The concept of shame could not remain intact if we subtract a concern for how our fellows view us, for feeling ashamed is just, in large measure, feeling lessened in the eyes of the reference group whose good opinion we value. This is revealed in the fact that primary shame behavior is *hiding* behavior, turning the face down or away, a point well made by Darwin in his important work *The Expression of the Emotions in Man and Animals.*[9]

Thus far, then, we get the following from Darwin: The moral sense or conscience of a human being will be, at least in part, a function of that being's social instincts—caring about others and especially caring about what those others think of us. Is this also *everything* to be said about conscience? Fortunately, Darwin answers *no* to this question, and he thereby avoids a theory of conscience that would be no less simplistic than that of Freud. Darwin well realizes that the conscience of any mature and civilized adult will involve more than simply a desire to help and be approved by one's fellows. At least two more things, he argues, are involved: *habit* and *reason*. The inclusion of habit on the list of the important items of moral psychology is interesting because here, by siding with Aristotle, Darwin throws one more punch at Kant who had offered a theory that made human action lose moral worth at the moment it became habitual and thus unreflective. But surely, Darwin argues, the very point of moral education is to make decent behavior a kind of "second nature" to the acting human being. As mentioned previously, too much Kantian agonizing, too much reflective "proing" and "conning", would, at least at certain stages of human development, have been an evolutionary disadvantage. Darwin writes:

I am aware that some persons maintain that actions performed impulsively . . . do not come under the dominion of the moral sense, and cannot be called moral. They confine this term to actions done deliberately, after a victory over opposing desires, or when prompted by some exalted motive. But it appears scarcely possible to draw any clear line of distinction of this kind. As far as exalted motives are concerned, many instances have been recorded of savages, destitute of any feeling of general benevolence towards mankind, . . . who have deliberately sacrificed their lives . . . rather than betray their comrades; and surely their conduct ought to be considered as moral. As far as deliberation, and the victory over opposing motives are concerned, animals may be seen doubting between opposed instincts, in rescuing their offspring or comrades from danger; yet their actions, though done for the good of others, are not called moral. Moreover, anything performed very often by us, will at last by done without deliberation or hesitation, and can then hardly be distinguished from an instinct; yet surely no one will pretend that such an action ceases to be moral. On the contrary, we all feel that an act cannot be considered as perfect, or as performed in the most noble manner, unless it be done impulsively, without deliberation or effort, in the same manner as by a man in whom the requisite qualities are innate. He who is forced to overcome his fear or want of sympathy before he acts, deserves, however, in one way higher credit than the man whose innate disposition leads him to a good act without effort. . . . [Thus, with respect to human beings,] actions of a certain class are called moral, whether performed deliberately, after a struggle with opposing motives, or impulsively through instinct, or from the effects of slowly-gained habit (Chap. IV, pp. 482–483).

Darwin thus once again shows himself capable of appreciating and even making a subtle kind of moral point. He agrees with Kant that there is a special kind of moral worth or value to be found in the reflective and deliberate overcoming of certain inclinations and habits; he clearly sees, however, that this admission does not force him to maintain that this is the only or even the unambiguously most important kind of moral value. One could stipulate such a limitation, of course, but this legislation about the use of the word "moral," in addition to being contrary to our common usage as Darwin correctly reports it, would enable us to make no point that could not be made in more modest ways. Kant, of course, wants to limit the moral realm to the realm of reflective deliberation because of his belief that, as participants in such a realm, human beings are freed from phenomenal causality and thus earn a special kind of moral dignity. Darwin will have none of this, and he sees no important reason for limiting the moral realm in a way that seems arbitrary and artificial.

Finally, we come to the moral role of *reason*. Though resisting any Kantian tendencies to regard reason as metaphysically spooky, Darwin does agree with Kant in regarding reason as a central element in human moral psychology, especially in the "advanced" moral psychology of "highly civilized" human communities. He writes:

At the present day civilised nations are everywhere supplanting barbarous nations, excepting where the climate opposes a deadly barrier; and they succeed mainly, though not exclusively, through their arts, which are the products of the intellect. It is therefore highly probable that with mankind the intellectual faculties have been mainly and gradually perfected through natural selection (Chap. V, p. 497).

Ultimately our moral sense or conscience becomes a highly complex sentiment—originating in the social instincts, largely guided by the approbation of our fellow-men, ruled by reason, self-interest, and in later times by deep religious feelings, and confirmed by instruction and habit (Chap. V, p. 500).

With civilised nations, as far as an advanced standard of morality, and an increased number of fairly good men are concerned, natural selection apparently effects but little; though the fundamental social instincts were originally thus gained (Chap. V, p. 504).

Thus moral sense [in part follows] from the high activity of [a human being's] mental faculties, with past impressions extremely vivid. . . . Owing to this condition of mind, man cannot avoid looking both backwards and forwards, and comparing past impressions. . . . The moral faculties are generally and justly esteemed as of higher value than the intellectual powers. But we should bear in mind that the activity of the mind in vividly recalling past impressions is one of the fundamental though secondary bases of conscience (Chap. XXI, p. 913).

The moral nature of man has reached its present standard, partly through the advancement of his reasoning powers and consequently of a just public opinion, but especially from his sympathies having been rendered more tender and widely diffused through the effects of habit, example, instruction, and reflection (Chap. XXI, p. 914).

Darwin's basic points about the moral role of reason, then, are these: (1) Reason is a crucial part of the moral life of all civilized human beings; (2) Reason is an instrumental faculty that allows human beings to compare present experiences with past experiences and to anticipate future experiences; it thus allows the introduction of deliberate planning, through trial and error, into the moral world of civilized human beings; (3) Though the faculty or instrument of reason was improved and developed through natural selection, the *actual use* of that faculty in particular circumstances is not biologically determined. Thus, to the degree that deliberate planning and education form a part of a creature's moral world, then to that same degree is the explanatory value of natural selection lessened. Natural selection might well have favored creatures with the capacity to be flexible, creative, and spontaneous in their responses to the world's challenges, but at this point the explanatory value of natural selection stops. For if one attempted to use the theory of natural selection (or any other determinist theory) to explain or predict the actual responses, this would be inconsistent with regarding them as flexible, creative, and spontaneous. Darwin thus openly admits that his theory of natural selection has only the most general explanatory value in accounting for a special part of the moral life of civilized human beings: rational reflection.

Up to this point, I have mainly been concerned to present a fair account of Darwin's views on morality and the moral sense. Before closing, however, I want to spend some time in the critical evaluation of those views. Darwin is not much fun to attack because he exhibits so much in the way of intellectual and academic virtue— i.e., he proceeds with great intellectual modesty and honesty, is tentative where, given the evidence, he should be tentative, and covers all that he does with a patina of personal charm and common sense. He is a genuinely civilized man. I do not propose to be deterred by this, however, since I believe that his views on morality, for all of their great insights, are still seriously defective in many important respects. Thus we shall temporarily abandon historical piety and shall treat Charles Darwin in much the same spirit as one might treat an anonymous scholar whose article one has been assigned to referee for possible publication in a contemporary journal. The case for acceptance "as is" will, I am afraid, be doubtful.

As a prelude to critical evaluation, let me note two distinctions of importance that Darwin generally observes but sometimes seems to forget. The first is a distinction between providing a natural or causal explanation for the emergence of a certain capacity or ability, on the one hand, and a natural or causal explanation for the particular exercises of that ability on the other. The second is a distinction between social evolution and biological evolution. These distinctions are of the first importance for, if they are not observed or are subtly collapsed in some way, then one can make the case for an evolutionary explanation of moral phenomena appear stronger than it is.

For example, suppose we wanted to attack Kant's view that human moral choice (rational autonomy) is special in some way that places it beyond ordinary patterns of biological explanation. We might make our case against this view appear quite illegitimately strong by noting, in quite general terms, that moral beliefs and practices have changed over time—i.e., that they have evolved. In so far as the term "evolution" means "descent with modification," the claim that moral beliefs and practices have evolved over time is hardly to be regarded as controversial. It is indeed a platitude. But the mere presence of evolution in some sense goes not one single step toward showing that the process of change is to be explained by factors that are in any sense biological. The evolution in question could be social in nature—explained, perhaps, as a result of a rational process of trial and error over time, whereby people drop or replace parts of their moral outlook that seem not to work or to be unfitted to new circumstances. This would be the kind of evolution exhibited, for example, by the common law, not by organisms, and thus would really have nothing to do with establishing the legitimacy of a biological perspective on the issues in question. Any selection here would be artificial and not natural, a point Darwin seems to miss when he mentions imprisonment and legal execution as selection factors in contemporary communities (Chap. V, p. 504).[10]

The rational process involved in social evolution may be seen, of course, as resting upon a capacity or ability (reason) that was developed and refined through a process of natural selection. But just because we can give a biological explanation of the presence or perseverence of a particular ability or capacity (to reason, to swim, to paint pictures, etc.), it does not follow that explanations of the particular uses of this ability are biological in nature. For example, one might explain a person's behavior by citing the fact that he *appreciated a rational argument*—e.g., he avoided exposing himself to frequent dental x-rays because he was presented with evidence that radiation causes genetic damage. It could be argued (though it is, of course, controversial) that the concept of appreciating a rational argument cannot be analyzed or understood in purely biological terms—that when behavior is explained in terms of responsiveness to reasons, it is not a biological explanation that is being given, but rather an explanation of a different logical or epistemological order. Perhaps it is not even a causal explanation. These views about explanation may be mistaken, but they are not incompatible with a belief that the capacity to reason (to appreciate the difference between good and bad reasons and to be motivated thereby) is to be explained, at least in part, in terms of the biological concept of natural selection. It is simply a fallacy to argue that, because reasoning abilities have survival value (and thus have persisted and been improved through a process of natural selection), reason explanations of action are themselves biological explanations. To put the point as simply as possible: just because there may be a biological explanation of how creatures acquired the capacity to do X, it does not follow that doing X is doing something biological or explainable in terms of the laws of biology. For even if reasoning involved a process of supernatural miracles, creatures endowed with this process would still have greater chances of survival than creatures not so endowed—the only point required by a theory of natural selection. Thus, insofar as a philosopher such as Kant may have been insisting primarily on the claim that reason explanations of action are different from ordinary causal (e.g., biological) explanations, his point will be untouched by the Darwinian claim that the presence, persistence, and improvement of the rational abilities found in human beings are to be explained biologically. Thus some important elements of the Kantian outlook might be more immune from the Darwinian assault than at first sight appeared. Even these elements may be unfounded—indeed, many able philosophers have argued that they are—but nothing in the Darwinian theory provides an argument that they are unfounded. If Kant limits his claim to maintaining that human behavior, unlike the behavior of other animals, is sometimes to be explained in terms of the concept of responding to reason, then his attempt to found human moral specialness on this feature, however controversial it may be on other grounds, is not refuted by anything that Darwin has to say. It is only if he wishes to insist on the much stronger point that the capacity or ability to respond to reason can in no sense be accounted for in terms of natural selection that the Darwinian theory will cause him trouble.

Now let us recall again just how limited in scope explanations in terms of natural selection really are. Take any capacity or ability. Natural selection alone cannot explain the nature of that ability or how that ability was originally introduced into the world. All it can do is explain why creatures having that ability (and increasingly improved refinements of that ability) stand a better chance of surviving than creatures lacking the ability or having an inferior and unrefined form of the ability. This is why Darwin, seeking to show the *descent* of man from lower animals, always supplements the argument from natural selection with massive data that tries to show striking analogies between human behavior and the behavior of other animals. As previously noted, he does this rather well for sociability, arguing that human sympathy is simply a refinement of feelings found in lower animals, differing from them only in degree and not in kind. But this kind of case cannot be made out so easily for human rationality. Admittedly rational behavior does occur in lower animals—e.g., an ape dealing with the problem of reaching some food by using a stick as a tool. Darwin's account of such cases in Chapter III is particularly rich and persuasive. And yet there *seem* to be elements of human rationality that differ in kind, and not just in degree, from the kinds of cases Darwin cites— e.g., such processes as responding to and weighing arguments pro and con on an issue (which *seems* to be more than simply being caught between competing impulses) and having what John Rawls calls "rational life plans" in terms of which one develops a vision of one's whole life (what it is and what it ought to be) and is motivated thereby. Also important in the rational process is what might be called *institutional* or *cultural behavior* (e.g., patriotism or draft evasion) where human beings at least seem to be motivated by seeing the *point* or *meaning* of what they do. All this may be an illusion and may be reduced to something quite biological in nature, but, if this is so, Darwin fails to show it. Sometimes he seems to think he has shown it, as when he writes as follows:

The high standard of our intellectual powers and moral disposition is the greatest difficulty which presents itself, after we have been driven to this conclusion on the origin of man. But every one who admits the principle of evolution, must see that the mental powers of the higher animals . . .

are the same in kind with those of man, though so different in degree (Chap. XXI, pp. 911–12).

But are they the "same in kind"? Just one page later, Darwin writes this:

A moral being is one who is capable of reflecting on his past actions and their motives; . . . and the fact that man is the one being who certainly deserves this designation is the greatest of all distinctions between him and the lower animals. . . . Hence after some temporary desire or passion has mastered his social instincts, he reflects and compares the now weakened impression of such past impulses with the ever-present social instincts; and he then . . . resolves to act differently in the future. . . . A pointer dog, if able to reflect on his past conduct, would say to himself, I ought (as indeed we say of him) to have pointed at that hare and not have yielded to the passing temptation of hunting it (Chap. XXI, pp. 912–13).

Look at what has been said in these nearly adjacent passages: (1) Reflection and resolve are the essential features of human moral psychology. (2) Other animals do not reflect and resolve, though they would be moral creatures *if* they did. This observation, especially when conjoined with those previously quoted passages where Darwin suggests that advanced civilizations transcend the biological and the mechanism of natural selection, indicates that Darwin was at least sometimes inclined to admit that the most special features of human beings are *not* open to biological explanation. But to admit this is to throw away one of the points of the chapters in question. Darwin's expressed views on this matter are really quite unclear, and one cannot help thinking that he just allowed himself to get very confused here. In so far as what is at work in culture is the rational mechanism of social evolution and artificial selection (e.g., imprisonment or legal execution), then what we have is simply not relevant to a work in *biology*. Extensive discussion of them in what is supposed to be a work in biology can only lead the reader to assume that Darwin himself might occasionally have neglected the two distinctions noted earlier between social and biological evolution and between explaining a particular piece of behavior and explaining the presence of the capacity to engage in such behavior.

Darwin, unlike Freud, had the good sense to admit complex features into his account of conscience or the moral sense, but he does not always seem to realize that those very features his good sense compels him to acknowledge are just the ones with which his biological theory is least equipped to deal.

Moving from the realm of moral psychology to the substantive content of morality (i.e., from conscience to sociability and sympathy) we find that Darwin here is also in similar trouble. He is forced by his good sense to admit into the moral world elements for which his biological theory is going to be hard-pressed to account. Occasionally, however, his errors here are even more serious—i.e., his good sense deserts him and he simply fails to recognize elements that any reasonable person would regard as morally important. These elements also happen to be ones for which a natural selection explanation seems implausible. There are also certain well-known empirical problems with his theory, but I shall here ignore them, beating a hasty retreat from issues in genetics upon which I cannot even fake a competent discussion.[11]

Let us return, then, to what Darwin has to say about the centrality of sociability and sympathy in morality. What does the fact of sociability and its involved instincts of sympathy have to do with moral principles? Darwin makes what we would now call a meta-ethical point—i.e., a point that is not itself normative moralizing, but is a point about normative moralizing, about the *concept of morality* itself. According to Darwin, we can discover from the evolved instincts what morality is about, what its essential content is—namely, it is essentially concerned with insuring that people can live together in communities in mutually supportive ways. What essentially makes an issue a moral issue (as opposed, say, to an aesthetic one) is that it is a problem in cooperative social living. Having said this, Darwin makes it clear that he does not believe that any *particular* principle for such regulation is biologically mandated. Particular principles of social cooperation will depend upon the particular natures of the cooperative beings and the environmental circumstances that face them.

If, for instance, to take an extreme case, men were reared under precisely the same conditions as hive-bees, there can hardly be a doubt that our unmarried females would, like the worker-bees, think it a sacred duty to kill their brothers, and mothers would strive to kill their fertile daughters; and no one would think of interfering (Chap. IV, p. 473).

As the legal philosopher H. L. A. Hart has pointed out: If we were born with crustacean-like exoskeletons, and were thus nearly unable to do each other damage, our moral notions of harm and benefit (and the moral centrality of the commandment not to kill) would be quite different from what they now are. This minimal point we can surely grant to natural law theory—a point quite consistent with wide divergence of actual moral principles and even with, as Hart notes, great iniquity.[12]

Sensible and insightful as this view is, however, it is too narrow, for the concept of morality is not reasonably to be limited to principles concerned with maintaining mutually supportive schemes of social cooperation. It may be the case that the core of morality is concerned with such matters, and it may also be the case that the centrality of such matters is a function of the biological nature of human beings, of the kinds of creatures we are. But the concept of morality is, of course, much broader than this—i.e., it includes (at least for many persons) such matters as personal moral virtue, integrity, and purity of heart. Even Darwin himself admits this and writes:

The highest possible stage in moral culture is when we recognize that we ought to control our thoughts, and "not even in inmost thought to think again the sins that made the past so pleasant to us" (Chap. IV, p. 492).

This admission shows good sense and a good grasp of the complexity and richness of the concept of morality, but it is by no means clear that the biological theory of natural selection provides a plausible explanation of this nonsocial dimension of morality.

An even more serious defect in Darwin's account of the concept of morality becomes clear when one considers his discussion of the moral theory of utilitarianism—the dominant secular moral philosophy of his day. The definitive feature of utilitarianism is the Principle of Utility as the supreme moral principle. The Principle of Utility states that, of all actions open to us, we are morally required to perform that action with the greatest tendency to maximize human happiness, "the greatest happiness for the greatest number" as Bentham put it. Darwin's responses to utilitarian theorists, especially J. S. Mill, are cogent and informed. Three are worth noting: (1) He regards Mill as having made a serious mistake in regarding all qualities of moral sentiment as being acquired rather than transmitted; (2) He sees the importance of distinguishing the motive of moral action from the standard of moral evaluation (Like

Mill, he realizes that one can act to promote the happiness of others without being motivated by the desire for happiness—one's own or theirs. One could act in this way out of instinct, habit, or a sense of duty.); and (3) He regards the utilitarian principle as too limited and narrow in characterizing human social morality in terms of the general happiness. He thinks instead that the notion of the general good or general welfare would give a clearer picture of the true nature of a socially beneficial code of conduct.

In the case of the lower animals it seems much more appropriate to speak of their social instincts, as having been developed for the general good rather than for the general happiness of the species. The term, general good, may be defined as the rearing of the greatest number of individuals in full vigour and health, with all their faculties perfect, under the conditions to which they are subjected. As the social instincts both of man and the lower animals have no doubt been developed by nearly the same steps, it would be advisable, if found practicable, to use the same definition in both cases, and to take as the standard of morality, the general good or welfare of the community, rather than the general happiness (Chap. IV, p. 490).

In spite of these quarrels of detail with utilitarianism, however, Darwin is basically a sympathetic follower of its primary teachings. He writes as follows:

Notwithstanding many sources of doubt, man can generally and readily distinguish between the higher and lower moral rules. The higher are founded on the social instincts, and relate to the welfare of others. They are supported by the approbation of our fellow-men and by reason. The lower rules . . . relate chiefly to self, and arise from public opinion, matured by experience and cultivation; for they are not practised by rude tribes (Chap. IV, p. 491).

But why are those moral rules relating to the welfare of others "higher" than other moral rules? Darwin seems to believe that they are because he regards nonaltruistic rules as little more than maxims for promoting self-interest, what Kant called counsels of prudence and banned from the moral realm. But surely this is a false dichotomy. There is certainly at least one important category of moral rules that, though certainly not altruistic, is certainly not reducible to prudential selfishness either. These rules are concerned, not with the promotion of group welfare at the possible expense of the individual, but with the *defense of the individual against the claims of the group.* I refer here to the moral rules usually thought of under such names as *rights, justice,* and *political liberty.* Someone who truly values, for example, the right of free speech may sometimes defend it even when he realizes that its exercise will not be in the best interest of the social group to which he belongs. Here we are concerned with the protection and promotion of self, certainly, but not in a merely prudential sense, for the concern with rights is not a concern with all exercises in self-promotion, but only in those that may be regarded as *legitimate.* The most important human rights, indeed, simply are concerned with protecting the sanctity of the individual against illegitimate group claims. This was an important insight of Kantian ethics that one might well want to retain even if one rejects totally the metaphysical foundation upon which he attempted to support it.

Unfortunately, this vital dimension of morality receives no attention or recognition at all from Darwin. And one can perhaps guess why this is so—namely, the origin of this kind of moral outlook is going to be much harder to explain on the basis of the theory sketched by Darwin in the chapters on morality. The concept of rights certainly evolved (e.g., we tend to make greater and different claims against our collective groups than was the case in the Middle Ages), but the evolution seems social rather than biological as the result of *thinking* about the oppressive nature of some collective claims and attempting to articulate theories and employ social experiments to develop less oppressive alternatives. These theories and experiments evolve socially (the common law is one of them), but there is nothing particularly biological at work in the process. Perhaps for this reason (or even perhaps because of a certain moral blindness encouraged by utilitarianism),[13] Darwin never faces up to the worry about the potentially oppressive nature of utilitarianism or any other theory stressing collective welfare—unless one gives a very generous interpretation to this one remark: "This definition [of moralty as the promotion of the general welfare] would perhaps require some limitation on account of political ethics" (Chap. IV, p. 490). To say the least!

Let me now summarize where we have reached to this point: I have argued that Darwin's concept of morality is much richer and more accurate than Freud's notion of morality as merely internalized parental commands. By stressing altruism (as acting for community good), he shows that morality has some reasonable social point and is not simply on a par with compulsive handwashing. His concept of morality is still too limited, however, for it stresses, without argument or justification, the "helping others" aspect of morality over the "protect the rights of the individual against the community" aspects. The whole liberal tradition that institutions exist for individuals and not the other way around is thus short-changed. One who is very sympathetic to the rights tradition would be interested in learning what, if anything, biological evolution can contribute to its understanding. Darwin, who seems not even to recognize it, is simply of no help here, and thus, for this reason, he cannot be said to have developed a complete theory of the origin of morality.

This brings me (at long last, I hear you sigh) to the end of my discussion of Darwin's views on the origins of morality and the moral sense. I have argued that his views exhibit some serious shortcomings, but I have also expressed admiration for the subtlety and profundity of many of his insights. He certainly deserves a far more serious attention from moral philosophers and the teachers of moral philosophy than he typically receives. Teachers of moral philosophy who want to make some gesture in the direction of the scientific or the nontraditional and thus expose their students to something outside the narrow confines of academic philosophy will frequently assign Freud's *Civilization and Its Discontents* or Nietzsche's *Genealogy of Morals*. The relevant chapters in *The Descent of Man* could, I think, be assigned with equal or even greater profit. Darwin has generally good sense and a powerful if limited theory. Contemporary sociobiologists, according to some of their critics, have neither. We shall examine that charge in the next chapter.

Notes

1. *Treatise*, Book II, Section III, Part III.

2. The appeal to the naturalistic fallacy can, of course, be overdone. It is correct to claim that moral principles are not directly derivable from statements of fact. On the other hand, it is utterly inconceivable that there could be *no* important connections between moral principles and the kind of creatures we in fact are—i.e., our human nature.

3. As a matter of prudence, of course, it is often unwise to interfere with the normal, and in that sense natural, course of things. Since, for

example, genetic mutations tend to be harmful or even lethal, one should be extremely cautious about introducing possible mutagens into the environment. The normal course of a tuberculosis infection, however, leads to death, and thus here a bit of interference with nature seems desirable—e.g., the use of some synthetic (and thus 'unnatural') drug perhaps.

4. There are dangers here, of course, that the claims of biological impossibility might be premature. If so, then in certain areas (e.g., racial and sexual discrimination) one might be tempted to mount a bogus biological argument in support of an unjustly repressive status quo. This is a good reason for always *presuming* biological possibility, thereby placing the burden of proof on the one who would seek to provide a biological foundation for a discriminatory classification.

5. For more on this, see my "Marxism and Retribution" in my *Retribution, Justice, and Therapy: Essays in the Philosophy of Law* (Dordrecht and Boston: D. Reidel, 1979).

6. See, for example, Kant's long and obscure footnote at 401–402 (Academy Edition) of his *Foundations for the Metaphysics of Morals.*

7. For more on autonomy, see my "Therapy and the Problem of Autonomous Consent," *International Journal of Law and Psychiatry* 2 (1979): 415–30.

8. All quotations from *The Descent of Man and Selection in Relation to Sex* are from the second edition of 1874. Since the compelling reasons for using the first edition of the *Origin* are not present with respect to the first edition of the *Descent*, I have used the second edition of the latter work because I tend to have a slight preference for its discussion of morality. The changes in the text of these chapters are few, but they tend to be small additions or amplifications that add clarity. Also, the organization of chapters in the second edition is clearly more logical. The pages given for the second edition are from the Random House Modern Library Giant volume *The Origin of Species* and *The Descent of Man.* (I used this volume because it is my experience that it is widely available in college and public libraries and in second-hand book stores.) Those readers desiring to consult the first edition of the *Descent* (published in 1871) will value the facsimile reproduction of that edition issued in 1981 by Princeton University Press. The chapters on morality in the first edition are numbered II, III, V, and XXI.

9. (Chicago: University of Chicago Press, 1965), pp. 320 ff. This work was first published in 1872.

10. James Le Maire (my very helpful copy editor on this volume) has pointed out to me that Darwin's occasional lack of clarity on the distinction between biological evolution and social evolution may be linked to his occasional lack of clarity on the degree to which he rejects the Lamarckian theory of the inheritance of acquired characteristics. Given their knowledge of genetics, most contemporary biologists reject Lamarckianism and see Darwinism as utterly at odds with it. The situation, of course, was not nearly so clear in Darwin's own day.

11. See Note 1 for Chapter 4.

12. Hart calls this the "minimum content of natural law" and discusses it at pp. 189 ff. of his *The Concept of Law* (Oxford: Oxford University Press, 1961).

13. John Alcock has suggested to me another reason for Darwin's neglect of individual rights—namely that, when he started thinking about morality, he got so carried away with a notion of group selection that he temporarily forgot that his general theory of natural selection involves the selection of *individuals* for *their own* survival and reproductive advantage. It is this "selfish" foundation that generates the problem of accounting for altruism in the first place, of course, and thus one must not become so charmed with one's account of altruism that one forgets the background of anti-altruism on which it rests. A concern with rights (protection of the individual against the group) clearly has a much stronger affinity with the "selfish" background than with the altruistic exceptions. Contemporary evolutionary biologists (including sociobiologists) tend to emphasize individual selection instead of group selection and thus are concerned to emphasize that altruistic behavior fits into an evolutionary perspective only to the degree that it confers survival and reproductive advantages upon individuals (or, more precisely, on the genes of those individuals). These contemporary writers see human groups as forming for the promotion of individual reproductive success, not the survival of the group as a whole, and thus are able to highlight the potential for conflict among individuals even within cooperative groups. Given this way of looking at the matter, these contemporary writers (e.g., E. O. Wilson) will be better able than Darwin to discuss preferences for rights in biological terms. Some of these issues will be explored in the following chapter. (For a clear and elementary discussion of group selection vs. individual selection, see Chapter 1 of Richard Dawkins' *The Selfish Gene*, Oxford: Oxford University Press, 1976.)

4

Sociobiology, Altruism, and the
Reduction of Morality

Scientists and humanists should consider together the possibility
that the time has come for ethics to be removed temporarily from the
hands of the philosophers and biologized.

E. O. WILSON

It would be as foolish to seek a biological evolutionary explanation
of ethics as it would be to seek such an explanation of physics.

THOMAS NAGEL

Whenever an individual considers a given [mental] process as being
too obvious to permit of any investigation into its origin, and shows
resistance to such investigation, we are right in suspecting that the
actual origin is concealed from him—almost certainly on account of
its unacceptable nature.

ERNEST JONES

Contemporary sociobiological theories are attempts to develop
biological explanations of all social behavior—human and nonhuman, moral and nonmoral. Insofar as they are concerned to explain
human moral behavior, they basically incorporate the Darwinian
theory of the origin of morality as outlined in the previous chapter.
They are generally more sophisticated than Darwin's account in
three important respects: (1) they rely on a genetic theory of kin-

selection in order to overcome certain empirical problems faced by an attempt to account for altruism in terms of natural selection;[1] (2) they generally involve a conception of human morality that is considerably more sophisticated than simple altruism; and (3) the defenders of these contemporary theories are more sensitive than Darwin (though often not sensitive enough) to the unique problems presented by dealing biologically with such concepts as rationality, intentionality and meaning, and culture. They generally realize that a few analogies drawn between human rationality and animal behavior will not be enough to meet the objections of someone who believes that human rationality, intentionality, and culture are *logically autonomous*—i.e., cannot, on logical or conceptual grounds, be reduced to something purely biological.

The theory of kin-selection has been ably discussed, both pro and con, in numerous well-known books and articles,[2] and I shall not attempt to transcend my competence and add to that discussion here. Instead I shall be concerned in this final chapter with the last two issues noted above. Taking the writings of E. O. Wilson as representative of the most interesting and persuasive statements of contemporary sociobiology as applied to morals,[3] I shall first explore the question of the degree to which his more sophisticated account is able to overcome the shortcomings noted in Darwin's original theory. As an outgrowth of this, I shall then explore the main question I wish to raise in this chapter: Is ethics or morality or moral philosophy logically autonomous—i.e., precluded, on logical or conceptual grounds, from being reduced, eliminated, undermined, or even affected by biological claims (either those presently being made by sociobiologists or any possible claims that sociobiologists might make in the future)? I am less concerned with the details of the Wilsonian enterprise than with the question of whether it is, as many humanist scholars would argue, *misconceived in principle*, as rather on a par with attempting to account for human morality in terms of carpentry or even astrology.

Focusing on this particular issue will, I think, allow me to do something many traditional humanists have no desire to do— namely, give sociobiology a sympathetic interpretation and bring out what is best and strongest in it. This will allow us to avoid the kind of "cheap shot" objections that philosophers can easily make against those outside of philosophy who attempt to develop theories with philosophical consequences, but who do not pay sufficient attention to our antiseptic terminological niceties. Wilson is—it must be acknowledged—sometimes outrageous in the extent to which he is willing to use the same concept (e.g., aggression, altruism, etc.) to describe both the behavior of animals in nature and humans in culture without even seeming to notice that there might be some serious problems involved in doing this (e.g., simple anthropomorphic projection). Or consider this remark by Gunther Stent: "All it would take for a culture-inclusive super-sociobiology of the future to connect that symbolic order with biology is a theory of meaning".[4] Well, yes, that is *all* it would take, but Stent seems not to realize that this might be quite a lot indeed and that many would argue, on conceptual grounds, that linguistic meaning is not the *kind* of thing that could in principle be accounted for in biological terms. Thus, not surprisingly, philosophers and anthropologists have taken sociobiologists to task for their cheerful optimism that the biological reduction of symbolic culture is just around the corner.

Such criticisms are important, of course, but simply to stop with them and to assume that one has thereby refuted Wilson and the whole sociobiological enterprise is to make a serious mistake. For three important points need to be made here.

(1) Theories cannot be discarded simply because they have problems—even very deep and serious problems. One must also consider what the possible alternative theories are. If they are plagued with difficulties identical with or even worse than those plaguing the theory under criticism, then the case for dismissing that theory (as opposed, say, to work at fixing it up) is weak. This point seems to me to be missed by such anthropological critics of sociobiology as Marshall Sahlins, for example.[5] In their zeal to insulate culture and meaning from biological explanation, they generate a theory of culture so ethereal as to insulate it from *all* explanation, even that of their own discipline of anthropology. If, as Hegel thought, culture represents the march of the Absolute Spirit through history, then it is of course true that culture will transcend biological explanation because it will transcend causal explanation of any kind. But if this only leaves us with Hegelian theories and explanations—history and culture as rational dialectic—then (as anyone who has ever tried to read Hegel will surely

agree) we might well want to have another shot at developing a biological account. Explanatory theories, in short, cannot be fully assessed in an isolated vacuum. We could, of course, disavow theory and simply intone such phrases as "culture" and "form of life" with reverential awe, but most of us are going to want some starting point or perspective from which to organize our further inquiry. And, given the imperfect world in which we live, we are likely to be forced to take, from all the possible theories before us, the one least defective, distorted, and crazy.

(2) Much creative progress in theoretical thought has been made by unusual or metaphorical extensions of common terms. Look, for example, at the moral breakthrough in our civilization when Socrates violated the conventions governing the concept of harm, redefined harm as *moral* injury, and gave sense to the claim that a good person cannot be harmed. And look at how much would have been lost had one simply said of Freud: "Unconscious thoughts? Of course not! Thoughts are not in principle the kind of thing that can be unconscious." Or recall the first review of Franck's *Symphony in D Minor:* "*That* a symphony? You can't have an English horn in a symphony!" In short, progress in thought and culture is not always served by spraying intellectual Lysol over the septic festering of terminological extension. Bernard Williams puts this point very nicely as follows:

[It is important to see the value of conceptual "slippage" because], of course, slippage in the application of a term is sometimes simply called generalization; there is an explanatory idea which underlies the use of the notion of "altruism" in both of these connections. To me that seems a very good reason for not being puritanically hygenic about the use of such terms. It is not just the psychological point . . . that it is difficult for most of us to think without slippage; it is that some valuable thought essentially involves slippage. It consists in generalizations of notions which have previously been used in a more restricted way.[6]

(3) It is important to distinguish what may be nonessential details or side excursions of a theory from its essential core. This is especially important when the excursions are attention-getters because, for example, they fit in with current social and political concerns. Remarks on race, gender, and sexual preference will be in this category, and what Wilson has to say on these matters could be defective without his essential program being undermined.

Wilson, of course, invites criticism here because of the generally sloppy way in which he casually develops his theory—mixing core claims with passing opinions and not taking Darwinian care in carefully distinguishing them. For example, he blithely defends two contradictory positions: ethical relativism (there are no universally objective values) and the view that we ought (absolutely and objectively, one presumes) control future human evolution in certain directions.[7] Here too, he has been properly criticized.[8] In my judgment, however, the person who is reading Wilson for ethical guidance—some crackerbarrel moral advice for the future from the perspective of evolutionary biology—will be reading him for what he is worst at and has the least to contribute. It is what he has to say about the nature of the enterprise of morality itself—i.e., his *meta-ethical* rather than his normative claims—that should be the focus of our attention. Beneath all of the jazzy remarks of journalistic appeal (remarks that have naturally received the most attention) there is what might be called Wilson's *deep theory:* a certain *general program* for ethics that transcends the particular details of current sociobiological accounts. This general program has positive arguments in its defense, but its starting point is an attack on the enterprise of moral philosophy itself—at least as that enterprise has been practiced within the dominant rationalist tradition. Wilson's strategy, in effect, is this: "There are two ways of going about an examination of ethics, my way (the biological way) and the other way (the way of the philosopher). I will show you— on biological grounds—the hopelessness of the philosophical way of proceeding. I will even show you that philosophical theories, when they are plausible, are tacitly assuming the very biological basis they officially reject. Given this, you ought to be willing to give sociobiology a fair hearing." As I interpret Wilson's most important contention, then, it is not to give us a positive normative theory, not to claim that he currently has at his disposal the biological apparatus to explain even the most complex features of symbolic culture, and certainly not to justify the current political *status quo.* It is rather to show, from the perspective of evolutionary biology, that traditional moral philosophy is a misconceived enterprise. Some evidence that I am correct in this interpretation is to be found in the fact that Wilson begins his book *On Human Nature* with a dismissal of moral philosophy by claiming that the work of two of its most illustrious contemporary practitioners, John Rawls and Robert Nozick, is simply inane.

Now I do not think that Wilson totally pulls off this project, for he by no means demonstrates that ethics would be in better hands if studied by biologists instead of philosophers. Rawls, for example, clearly offers something of great value I doubt that any biologist could equal—namely, a careful and profound analysis of various moral concepts and a highly plausible account of how these concepts may fit together in a systematic and ordered whole. However, on the issue of foundations for ethics, the role of "proof" in moral philosophy, Wilson is on firmer ground. Indeed, his case here, if properly reconstructed with the help of sympathetic philosophers, is very serious and deserves more consideration from moral philosophers. (It certainly deserves better than the offhand dismissal it often receives at the hands of "humanists.") His account belongs, I think, in the camp with those developed by Hume, Nietzsche, Marx, and Freud—thinkers concerned to persuade us that all is not rosy in the world of rationalistic moral philosophy.

This is not, of course, the way that Wilson is normally interpreted by philosophers. Typically, and many of his remarks justify this, he is viewed as in the Aristotelian camp of ethical naturalism—i.e., as one who attempts to show that the basic principles of morality will be discovered through an examination of human nature rather than in an *a priori* Platonic manner. Though it is typical to dismiss such Aristotelian theories by crying "Naturalistic Fallacy!" (rather as a referee might call "Foul!"), I am myself by no means persuaded by this hasty dismissal, for I find it inconceivable that there could be *no* important connections between morality and the kind of creatures we are. Still, insofar as Wilson is interpreted in this way, he has nothing very new to contribute to a very old philosophical debate—what he says here being much better said by earlier philosophers.

At his best, Wilson is not so much an ethical naturalist as an *ethical relativist,* and his foundations for such relativism, though having many affinities with older traditions, are also novel in many ways. He may be making good on the unsupported guess made by Nietzsche in *Beyond Good and Evil* when he speculated that "physio-psychology" was the road to moral understanding and wrote:

It is high time to replace the Kantian question, "How are [*a priori* moral judgments] possible?" by another question, "Why is belief in such judgments *necessary*?"—and to comprehend that such judgments must be *believed* to be true, for the sake of the preservation of creatures like ourselves; though they might, of course, be *false* judgments for all that! . . . After having looked long enough between the philosopher's lines and fingers, I say to myself: by far the greater part of conscious thinking must still be included among instinctive activities, and that goes even for philosophical thinking. We have to relearn here, as one has had to learn about heredity and what is "innate." . . . "Being conscious" is not in any decisive sense the opposite of what is instinctive: most of the conscious thinking of a philosopher is secretly guided and forced into certain channels by his instincts.[9]

Compare this with Wilson in *On Human Nature*:

Like everyone else, philosophers measure their personal emotional responses to various alternatives as though consulting a hidden oracle. That oracle resides in the deep emotional centers of the brain, most probably within the limbic system, a complex array of neurons and hormone secreting cells located just below the "thinking" portion of the cerebral cortex. Human emotional responses and the more general ethical practices based on them have been programmed to a substantial degree by natural selection over thousands of generations.[10]

Or consider this passage from *Genes, Mind, and Culture*—a book that Wilson co-authored with Charles J. Lumsden:

A society that chooses to ignore the implications of the innate epigenetic rules will still navigate by them and at each moment of decision yield to their dictates by default. Economic policy, moral tenets, the practices of child rearing, and virtually every other social activity will continue to be guided by inner feelings whose origins are not examined. Such a society must consult but cannot effectively challenge the oracle residing within the epigenetic rules. It will continue to live by the "conscience" of its members and by "God's will." Such an archaic procedure might lead in the most direct and untroubled manner to a stable and thoroughly benevolent culture. More likely, it will perpetuate conflict and relentlessly drag humanity along what is at best a tortuous and dangerous path. On the other hand, the deep scientific study of the epigenetic rules will call the oracle to account and translate its commands into a precise language that can be understood and debated. Societies that know human nature in this way might well be more likely to agree on universal goals within the constraints of that nature. And although they cannot escape the inborn rules of epigenesis, and indeed would attempt to do so at the risk of losing the very essence of humanness, societies can employ knowledge of the rules to guide individual behavior and cultural evolution to the ends upon which they agree.[11]

Wilson, like Nietzsche, is "doing philosophy with a hammer." Sloppy and undisciplined as some of his speculations are, they constitute a broad scale attack that is extremely valuable in allowing us to gain a new perspective on the nature of our ethical activities—a perspective that can be valuable (even if it turns out to be wrong or seriously limited) in that it shows us where our moral theories are vulnerable and the weaknesses in our views that we have either been ignoring or about which we have been deceiving ourselves. Thus my goal here is to give the Wilsonian perspective a sympathetic run for its money. My ultimate conclusion is that it is by no means the whole story about ethics (philosophers may still remain in business[12]), but that it has a greater relevance for ethical theory than many of its often hysterical humanist detractors have been willing to see or admit.

In order to start the process of viewing Wilson sympathetically, let me note the ways in which (in my judgment) he has made advances over Darwin in his treatment of the origins of morality. Recall that I had two main objections to make to Darwin's account: (1) Darwin had no plausible way of linking up biology with the admitted role of reason or rationality in the moral life; and (2) Darwin viewed morality as simply a matter of promoting the general welfare—i.e., he was an uncritical utilitarian and thus made no place for the role of such moral concepts as *rights, desert,* and *justice,* concepts concerned to defend the individual against the claims of the group.

Sketchy as Wilson's views on these matters are, they still (in my judgment) represent advances over what Darwin had to say. Indeed, just noticing that there are important issues and problems here is itself an advance. First, consider the issue of rationality in ethics. Wilson does not say that each instance of rational moral behavior can be reduced to an instance of acting on instinct or some other primitive biological process. He is no simplistic reductionist with respect to reason and culture and thus does not maintain—what is probably false and is surely unsupportable at present—that there is some simple isomorphism between human biological needs and particular actions within complex intellectual and cultural systems (including moral systems). No, the claim for biological foundations is more subtle than this—which is why I prefer to think of Wilson as an anti-inflationist instead of a reductionist—and goes something like this: Of course, a complex intellectual and cultural activity such as morality involves a rather complex process of reason exchange (moral discourse and argument) having its own internal logic and which, *at that level*, is ludicrous to describe in biological terms. However, such a process will typically involve a hierarchical rational structure: reasons supported by more basic reasons in turn supported by even more basic or primitive reasons—a process finally reaching a stopping point at a set of pretheoretical convictions that cannot themselves be rationally defended because they are definitive for rationality in this particular domain. But where do these primitive "intuitions" come from, and why do we dig in our heels and cling to them and the structures they define at all costs? It is here, says Wilson, that biology has something to teach us.

Wilson may be wrong on this, but the view is no simple-minded reductionism and thus cannot be dismissed with a few offhand arguments. Consider the nature of his attack on a particular edifice of reason in the realm of moral philosophy—the theory of justice articulated and defended by John Rawls in his *A Theory of Justice.* How, in Rawls' judgment, is his theory to be proved superior to all competing moral theories? The answer Rawls gives is explained through a technical device he calls *reflective equilibrium.* According to Rawls, a theory puts us in the desirable and theory-confirming state of reflective equilibrium if it does a better job than any other theory of embracing and ordering the largest possible subset of our pretheoretical convictions about what is good and evil, right and wrong, just and unjust. *But where do these convictions come from and what is their status in justification*—i.e., *why do we place so much confidence in them?* Wilson and other sociobiologists are, I think, dead right in wanting to ask this question and dead right in thinking that an honest answer to it will unmask, at least partially, some of the pretensions of moral philosophy. If these convictions can be shown to be simply the result of biological instincts preserved in evolution by natural selection, then their status in moral epistemology will be affected. For moral theory would then be *relativized* to a degree that many of the "New Deontologists" in ethics—Rawls, Nozick, Fried, Dworkin—would no doubt find objectionable. The view of reason adopted by sociobiology is Humean and regards it as an *instrument* that allows us to calculate the best means to the attainment of our ends. It can even evaluate ends when these are seen as subordinate to even higher or more important ends. What it cannot do, however, is evaluate the ends finally accepted as ultimate, for these are given by the passions and, at this level, reason is the slave of the passions. And where do these basic passions come from? Evolutionary biology surely has at least part of the answer to this question.[13]

As Aristotle pointed out long ago in rejecting Plato's ethical intellectualism, an adequate moral theory must be able to account for *moral motivation*—for the fact that we care about moral requirements and that they move us to act. Only an account of morality grounded in the passions (the good as object of desire or, as Aristotle put it, as "that at which things aim") will be able to account for motivation, and the price for this, of course, will be a kind of relativism. Indeed, this dilemma has always been at the heart of moral philosophy. Take an intellectualist or rationalistic approach (the good as an object of cognition) and you will get universal objectivity (or at least a pretty good illusion of it), but you will not be able to account for moral motivation—attending to the good as an object of knowledge being quite compatible, of course, with being indifferent to it in feeling and action. Take an emotive approach (the good as an object of desire) and you will be able to explain moral motivation, but you will be stuck with a relativistic account of morality—relativized to the contingent facts of human nature, particularly facts about patterns of desire and preference. Thus, the two things we want most in ethics, universal objectivity and motivation, are perhaps incompatible.

Sociobiology is willing to sacrifice the universal objectivity for a plausible theory of motivation and preference and is thus willing to pay the price of a kind of relativism, though of a rather sophisticated kind. The thesis is not that each particular moral judgment describes or evinces a particular biological need or instinct—it is not *that kind* of relativism, the simple-minded kind we all know how to refute in our introductory ethics courses. Rather it is what might be called *relativism at the level of theory or proof*. The sociobiologist can admit that particular moral judgments are immediately derivable or supportable from a variety of different sources, culture, religion, even moral theory. Where biology comes in is to explain the nature of those sources. The particular judgment may be derivable from the theory; however, the theory itself is supported, not by some wider or more general theory, but by certain facts of human biology. In short, at the most ultimate level support becomes *causal* rather than rational. This by no means entails that morality becomes worthless or meaningless, of course, but only that moral values are ultimately relativized to the facts of human nature. But relative values are still values.

Let me expand a bit on the notion of relativism I am using here. In Chapter 1, I called Hume and Nietzsche ethical or moral *skeptics.* What were they skeptical about? The existence of moral values? Surely not, because both gave theories about the causal origin of such values; and how can one give a causal account of something when one does not accept the existence of that thing? The skepticism involved is rather about a certain common philosophical (and theological) account of the nature of such values—namely, that they are universal, objective, and provable truths. The strongest such account in this tradition is that provided by Kant who regarded the claims of morality as even more universally objective than those of science. Kant claimed that moral judgments are true, not merely of this actual world, but for all possible worlds containing rational beings. The ethical skeptic, therefore, will naturally take Kant and his followers to constitute the most powerful enemy camp.

Given that the ethical skeptic accepts the existence of values, but given also that he rejects the concept of values as universal objective truths, what account of the nature of values might he then accept? One account for which he would have a natural affinity is some form of *relativism:* values are not universal objective truths, but are rather expressions of the preferences of persons or groups of persons. (Consider a simple example: "Water is a combination of hydrogen and oxygen" is a statement the truth of which is utterly independent of human belief, desire, or preference. "Theft is morally wrong" is not, according to the position of relativism, a statement of comparable universal objectivity. It is not independent of the beliefs, desires, and preferences of people, but is indeed an expression of those beliefs, desires, and preferences. There is a sense in which "thinking makes it so" is true of the moral realm.) Values can vary because persons and their preferences can vary; and thus in this sense values are relativized to persons and their preferences—their *nature*, in short. An inquiry into the causal origin of values will, on this view, be an inquiry into the origins of certain patterns of preference—exactly the kind of inquiry we find in Hume, Darwin, Nietzsche, Freud, and Wilson.

Let me give an example here: one might quite naturally ask the questions "Why is incest wrong?" or "Why do people believe incest is wrong?" or "Why do most people have a strong preference against incest—i.e., a strong tendency to disapprove of incest and avoid it (or feel guilty if they do not avoid it)?" (If one is at all persuaded by sociobiology, one will not see these as totally separate questions.) There are, of course, all sorts of answers one could give, from "God forbids incest" to "There is an incest taboo—a culturally generated prohibition designed to curtail sexual jealousy and rivalry within the family." These answers all involve citing a *reason*, something of which persons opposing incest could even be aware and cite to justify their disapproval of incest.

But could there be a biological basis, a *cause*, for the general human avoidance of incest? We now know, of course, that inbreeding is genetically harmful; but this, it might be argued, could not be the basis of the incest taboo because the taboo is found universally, even among primitive people with no understanding of genetics or indeed any science at all. The sociobiologist, however, will say that such rejection is too hasty and superficial. Since inbreeding is genetically harmful, they would argue, those animals having a tendency to avoid incest would tend to produce healthier offspring than those indulging in incest. Thus (as Wilson suggests in *On Human Nature*) it is easy to see how, through natural selection over many generations, those having a preference against incest would far outnumber those not having this preference. Thus the actual causal basis for a preference against incest would be biological; and the cultural taboo might be no more than an epiphenomenon, a covering rationale (or perhaps additional reinforcer) developed after the fact. If this account is correct, of course, then one would expect to see in nonhuman animals a tendency to avoid incest also; and, indeed, such recent studies as John L. Hoogland's "Prairie

Dogs Avoid Extreme Inbreeding" (*Science*, March, 1982) indicate that such a tendency is indeed present. Thus our human cultural norms prohibiting incest may ultimately be based in biology— relativized to our animal nature after all.

This kind of moral relativism strikes many persons as disquieting, even dangerous. (Some "scientific creationists" push this pattern of reasoning: Evolution leads to atheism leads to moral relativism leads to drugs, sex, violence, and lack of patriotism.) The worry is this: if values boil down to preferences, and if preferences can change, then is it not simply a matter of good *luck* that there is currently a great deal of human agreement (and thus moral stability) with respect to matters of value? And if this is so, might not our luck change for the worse at any moment—i.e., might not preferences become hopelessly diverse with resulting moral (and even social) anarchy? Lucky for us, Hitler-type preferences are now in a minority. How do we know that tomorrow they will not become dominant?

If one's perspective on this matter is Darwinian, then one will not be so worried by the above expressions of fear; for on the Darwinian view the existing patterns of preference are *not* a matter of luck, but are rather the result of a long selection process that made them similar, settled, and firm. If there is any problem for the Darwinian view it is in making place for moral creativity, difference, and change—not in making place for stability. In part because of the evolutionary development of morality, it is to be expected that morality would be on the whole a highly conservative institution; for evaluative experimentation is not productive of stability and thus would not have had (at least at most points in human history) any survival value. To the extent, therefore, that our moral views incorporate their evolutionary history (as Bertrand Russell once said that our metaphysical views incorporate those of the Stone Age), we should not expect radical change to come from within the moral realm. Perhaps Nietzsche was right: If we want to move on to higher levels of personal grandeur, excellence, and achievement, this will require an inversion of values—a transcending or suspending of our ordinary, repressive moral and ethical preferences. Our evolutionary history will probably fight us on this (and will probably win), for Nietzschean "self-overcoming" will require an overcoming of at least part of our evolutionary history, a task for which (for obvious causes) that history has not prepared us. Thus conservatives need not fear evolution nearly as much as they should fear those who would seek to overcome evolution and the inherent factors of stability and similarity it has produced. In short: To have values relativized to the evolved patterns of human preference that constitute our human nature is by no means to have values rendered arbitrary, capricious, and unpredictable. If anything, it renders them too conservative and rigid. As I shall argue below in my discussion of rights, there are perhaps good evolutionary reasons in favor of social structures that allow even considerable individuality, spontaneity, and free play with respect to *actions* by members of a group. Since such freedoms will presumably be defended and enforced by internal and external moral sanctions, however, it is not at all clear that evolution would favor *moral* or *evaluative* freedom, disagreement, and spontaneity. At this point, of course, all these matters are highly speculative.

Having explored the issues of reason and relativism in the context of sociobiology, let us now move to the problem of rights and utility. Here Wilson's views also seem to me to represent some advance over those expressed by Darwin. Contrary to what is often said about sociobiology, Wilson does *not* identify human morality with simple altruism or group-beneficial behavior. There is much of this in human morality, of course, but Wilson suggests other features that at least seem to be in the same camp as concerns about rights and justice. He writes as follows:

Universal human rights might properly be regarded as . . . a primary value. The idea is not general; it is largely the invention of recent European-American civilization. I suggest that we will want to give it primary status not because it is a divine ordinance . . . or through obedience to an abstract principle of unknown extraneous origin, but because we are mammals. Our societies are based on the mammalian plan: the individual strives for personal reproductive success foremost and that of his immediate kin secondarily; further grudging cooperation represents a compromise struck in order to enjoy the benefits of group membership. A rational ant—let us imagine for a moment that ants and other social insects had succeeded in evolving high intelligence—would find such an arrangement biologically unsound and the very concept of individual freedom intrinsically evil. We will accede to universal rights because power is too fluid in advanced technological societies to circumvent this mammalian imperative; the long-term consequences of inequity will always be visibly dangerous to its temporary beneficiaries. I suggest that this is the true reason for the universal rights movement and that an understanding of its raw biological causation will be more compelling in the end than any rationalization contrived by culture to reinforce and euphemize it.[14]

In spite of some shortcomings to be noted a bit later, there is, I think, a core insight present in these remarks about justice and rights—namely, that these are devices for staking out protected areas of territory and activity (what Nozick calls "moral space") whereby each person can legitimately pursue his or her own interests in general independence of group claims. The group as a whole may benefit, of course, from allowing such rights to its members; for it is thereby better able to draw on their creativity and spontaneity than it would be in a coerced or otherwise rigid system of social control. Culturally complex creatures may derive survival advantage from novelty and invention, and thus they may benefit from those looser social structures that allow this kind of free play. However, as Wilson notes, these social benefits will not be the reasons motivating individuals to claim rights; these reasons will be more self-interested in nature—the altruism here (as Darwin himself noted[15]) being *reciprocal altruism*. The derivative social benefits will be explained in a way rather like Adam Smith's idea that the free pursuit of individual advantage produces group benefit. What drives each individual to seek a system of rights, then, is something basic in that individual's biological nature— what Wilson calls the "mammalian plan."

What does Wilson mean by this? He explains it with his distinction between what he calls "hardcore altruism" (found, for example, in insects) and "softcore altruism" (found in mammals):

We must distinguish two basic forms of cooperative behavior. The altruistic impulse can be irrational and unilaterally directed at others; the bestower expresses no desire for equal return and performs no unconscious actions leading to the same end. I have called this form of behavior "hard-core" altruism, a set of responses relatively unaffected by social reward or punishment beyond childhood. Where such behavior exists, it is likely to have evolved through kin selection or natural selection operating on entire, competing family or tribal units. We would expect hard-core altruism to serve the altruist's closest relatives and to decline steeply in frequency and intensity as relationship becomes more distant. "Soft-core" altruism, in contrast, is ultimately selfish. The "altruist" expects reciprocation from society for himself or his closest relatives. His good behavior is calculating, often in a wholly conscious way, and his maneuvers are orchestrated by the excruciatingly intricate sanctions and demands of society. The capacity for soft-core altruism can be expected to have evolved primarily by selection of individuals and to be deeply influenced by the vagaries of cultural evolution. . . . [In] human beings soft-core altruism has been carried to elaborate extremes. Reciprocation among distantly related or unrelated individuals is the key to human society.[16]

Even considered purely as a causal account, these remarks of Wilson's are highly problematical. One wonders, for example, why rights-based-on-reciprocation is an "invention of recent European-American civilization" if the basis for rights preference is in fact encoded in all mammals. If this latter claim is true, one would naturally expect the human rights movement to have a much longer and more universal history. It is thus incumbent upon Wilson to give a biological account for the absence of the universality his theory would lead one to expect. He may have such an account in mind when he suggests that the "fluidity of power" is a relevant factor bearing on the emergence of rights; however, this thought is too vague to be of very much help here. Not only is the notion of fluidity of power intrinsically unclear, but Wilson also claims that such fluidity is a property of "advanced technological societies"—not a causal property that is obviously biological in nature. Problems compound when Wilson asserts that the development of a preference for rights evolved "primarily by selection of individuals and . . . deeply influenced by the vagaries of cultural evolution." This begins to sound very much like *artificial selection*, not natural selection, and one begins to wonder what all the talk about "the mammalian plan" now really comes to. This is all pretty fuzzy, and even Wilson's most ardent admirers must surely admit that he has at most given us a very tentative *start* toward a partial biological account of the development of a human preference for rights. (A start, of course, is something; and none of the problems I have noted show that his search is misguided in principle.)[17]

There are, of course, those who will say that my expressed sympathy for Wilson's enterprise (even though the sympathy is highly qualified) represents a colossal, even embarrassingly naive, misunderstanding of the nature of moral philosophy. They will claim that moral philosophy is logically autonomous and thus is in principle invulnerable to being affected by biological claims. An interesting defense of this autonomy thesis has been presented by the philosopher Thomas Nagel, and I would like briefly to comment on his arguments and explain why, in my judgment, they do not work.

In his essay "Ethics as an Autonomous Theoretical Subject,"[18] Nagel argues that biology is in principle useless to the philosophical study of ethics. He offers three basic reasons in support of this claim—none of them in my judgment terribly persuasive.

(1)Moral philosophy has an internal logic (an internal set of standards of justification) that insulates it from external criticism. It is no doubt true that philosophy does have its own internal standards of procedure and justification that define it as philosophy. These certainly shield it from philosophical criticism, but *not* from external criticism in general. Such criticism will involve challenging those very standards and procedures or their presuppositions. To use a somewhat unfair but not utterly inapt analogy: the belief in Santa Claus has its own internal logic—rules of the "Santa Claus game" that distinguish correct from incorrect things to say about Santa Claus and his behavior. For example, it is true (internally to the Santa Claus game) that Santa Claus brings toys to nice children on Christmas; it is false (internally again) that she brings pumpkins to puppies on Easter. The possibility of making these and other equally profound internal moves does not in the least, however, insulate the whole Santa Claus enterprise from external criticism and rejection—a process that no doubt most of us in this culture have gone through at least once in our lives. Thus simply because morality has an internal logic, it does not follow that it may not be externally attacked from without by (for example) biology. The attack will not be philosophical (will not follow those rules), but will rather be an attack on the presuppositions of philosophy; and philosophy is not so wonderfully self-confirming and self-justifying as an activity as to simply brush these attacks off.

(2) We would regard the reduction of mathematics and physics to biology as absurd; thus too should we regard the reduction of ethics to biology as comparably absurd. I have already expressed my own doubts about

the reduction (in every sense) of ethics to biology, about its merits and about it as a correct description of Wilson's enterprise. I find it very difficult, however, to see what Nagel's particular *reason* against reduction comes to. It may be a version of point (1) above and open to the same objections. It may be the claim that mathematics and physics, being in some sense more basic sciences, cannot be reduced to a science (biology) less basic. (If anything, biology might be reduced to mathematics or physics.) But on this interpretation, the analogy with ethics breaks down. For ethics is not a more basic science (i.e., nobody is going to suggest that biology could be reduced to ethics) because ethics is not in the same sense a science at all. The basic point, then, is perhaps simply this: ethics is a process of reason and thought and "we have no general biological understanding of human thought."[19] But this criticism is question begging. Of course we do not yet have such an understanding, for the very point of sociobiology is the attempt to generate a theory that will provide this. If one could show that this attempt is wrong in principle, then that would be a fatal blow to the biological enterprise; but this cannot be shown merely by noting that we in fact now lack such an account.

(3)The claims of sociobiology are either trivial or false. It is natural to see why Nagel might make this charge because it is true of much that Wilson and other sociobiologists have to say. Often they write as though they (and not Aristotle) had first thought of attempting to ground ethical principles in human nature, had invented the metaphysical doctrine of determinism, and had been the first to attempt to prove this doctrine from the facts of science. Here one is inclined to follow the critic who once said of a new book: "It contains much that is new and much that is true. Unfortunately, what is new is not true; and what is true is not new." But, as I have previously suggested, this is not the best way to read sociobiology for its best insights. Even Nagel, for example, is prepared to concede this much:

Ethics . . . [involves] . . . communal activities of criticism, justification, acceptance, and rejection. . . . It begins . . . with prereflective ideas about what to do, how to live, and how to treat other people. . . . Biology may tell us about [these] perceptual and motivational starting points, but in its present state it has little bearing on the thinking process by which these starting points are transcended.[20]

Admitting this, in my judgment, is to admit a great deal. If our ethical theories are ultimately grounded in basic pretheoretical intuitions or convictions (i.e., if the data of philosophical ethics must be actual moral beliefs); and if ethical theory develops through a process still deeply involving these beliefs (i.e., if we are committed, for example, to getting reflective equilibrium by retaining the largest consistent set of them); and if the roots of these "starting points" (and, it would seem, finishing points also) are biological; then biology surely does have *some* bearing on these theories because the starting points are in fact never ultimately transcended. That they are is an illusion.

Let me put the point as simply as possible: Nagel claims that moral philosophy is autonomous from biology, but that actual moral beliefs and practices are not. But, insofar as he agrees with the Rawlsian account of moral philosophy as developing theories tested in part against our moral beliefs, he has simply fallen into inconsistency. Thus neither morality nor moral philosophy has been shown to be autonomous in Nagel's sense.[21]

If we view sociobiology as a critical reflection on the nature and foundations of moral philosophy, as an attack on its insulated criteria of theoretical adequacy, it is by no means clear that Nagel's arguments assure that moral philosophy is invulnerable to certain consequences of this reflection. Moral philosophy is somewhat relativized and humbled and can no longer seek to replace religion and speak as the voice of timeless and eternal reason. In trying to replace religion here, philosophy is simply filling a much needed gap.[22]

Let me summarize: I have not been concerned here to present a positive defense for sociobiology, but have rather been concerned to establish two much more modest claims: (1) its contemporary forms (e.g., the version presented by Wilson) represent sophisticated advances in moral thinking over what Darwin had to offer; and (2) and most important, its application to moral philosophy is not clearly mistaken in principle. Wilson's deep suspicions about moral philosophy may be justified, and his own program may give us valuable insights into morality. It is presumptuous of moral philosophers simply to assume otherwise. My moral then is simple: I welcome sociobiologists into the area of moral thinking and am happy to admit, even hope, that their research may provide us with insights of value.[23]

Notes

1. The chief empirical problem is explicitly noted by Darwin in *The Descent of Man:* "But it may be asked, how within the limits of the same tribe did a large number of members first become endowed with these social and moral qualities, and how was the standard of excellence raised? It is extremely doubtful whether the offspring of the more sympathetic and benevolent parents, or of those who were the most faithful to their comrades, would be reared in greater numbers than the children of selfish and treacherous parents belonging to the same tribe. He who was ready to sacrifice his life, as many a savage has been, rather than betray his comrades, would often leave no offspring to inherit his noble nature" (Chap. V, pp. 498–99). In short, the problem is this: If I have strong social or altruistic instincts and thus run risks for others, my chances of individual survival are less than the chances of a truly selfish person. Thus my chances of leaving progeny are less. Thus it would seem that altruists, instead of being selected, would be weeded out in evolutionary competition.

Darwin himself makes some clever attempts to meet this objection—e.g., by postulating (Chap. V, p. 499) a notion of self-benefiting reciprocity. An even more persuasive attempt, however, is the recent theory of genetic kin-selection developed by W. D. Hamilton and adopted by Wilson and others. According to this theory, a person who will sacrifice for the benefit of his kin will have a greater chance of having his genes survive than a person who does not, and thus there is natural selection value (at the genetic level) of sympathetic behavior even if it involves self-sacrifice. This still leaves the problem of how we may account, in evolutionary terms, for sacrifice for nonrelatives who are still members of one's group. Here we might have to fall back on Darwin's notion of reciprocity.

2. For a philosophically interesting discussion of kin-selection see Chapter 8 of Alexander Rosenberg's *Sociobiology and the Preemption of Social Science* (Baltimore: Johns Hopkins University Press, 1980).

3. Wilson has written three books of interest to the moral philosopher: *Sociobiology: The New Synthesis* (Cambridge: Harvard University Press, 1978); *On Human Nature* (Cambridge: Harvard University Press, 1978); and (with Charles J. Lumsden) *Genes, Mind and Culture* (Cambridge: Harvard University Press, 1981). See also R. D. Alexander's *Darwinism and Human Affairs* (Seattle: University of Washington Press, 1979), and Richard Dawkins' *The Selfish Gene* (Oxford: Oxford University Press, 1976).

4. *Morality as a Biological Phenomenon,* Gunther S. Stent, ed. (Berkeley: University of California Press, 1980), p. 6.

5. See Marshall Sahlins, *The Use and Abuse of Biology; An Anthropological Critique of Sociobiology* (Ann Arbor: University of Michigan Press, 1976).

6. *Supra* note 4, p. 276.

7. See, for example, p.6 of *On Human Nature* where Wilson suggests that someday we will have to grab hold of our destinies and "decide how human we wish to remain." But by what standard are we to make this

decision given that, according to Wilson, all standards are rooted in that very nature we may seek to transcend?

8. See Chapter 9 of Michael Ruse's excellent book *Sociobiology: Sense or Nonsense?* (Dordrecht and Boston: D. Reidel, 1979). When I speak of Wilson's "relativism," I am referring to his view that moral judgments are relative to the biological nature of the human species. Moral judgments could thus make (or rest upon) objective claims *about such creatures* without being objective or absolute in Kant's sense—i.e., without being true for all possible rational beings (whatever that means).

9. Pt. I, secs. ll and 3. The influence of Darwin on Nietzsche is obvious. His expressed contempt for Darwin may be a part of his compulsion to express contempt for all things English.

10. P. 6.

11. Pp. 358–60.

12. "But doing *what?*" I hear you ask. The question is not as difficult to answer as one might think. Though philosophers should abandon their attempt to speak as the voice of eternal moral wisdom and likewise their attempt to prove ethical theories, there is still very much of value to be done in the way of conceptual analysis and establishing systematic connections between moral concepts. Could anyone, for example, seriously believe that Rawls' work is without profound value just because his proofs fail to work? Anyone who reads *A Theory of Justice*, I submit, is going to be able to think about morality in a more sophisticated way because of it.

13. It perhaps does not have the whole answer, however. Just because our pretheoretical convictions are present because of causal factors prior to any moral theory, it does not follow that these causal factors must be biological. Marxists, for example, criticize Rawls' theory because of the belief that it builds into its very structure a certain social class bias—i.e., that it will put members of only certain social classes into the position of reflective equilibrium. If this is correct, then the sociobiologists can maintain their emphasis on the biological only by developing a biological theory of social class—a task in which studies of insect societies may prove useful. Another related problem is this: if moral theories appeal to us only because they capture certain of our innate biological preferences, how does one account for the incredibly large number of different theories abroad in the world on moral matters, all with adherents who presumably have their intuitions or pretheoretical convictions satisfied thereby? Western liberals will be high on theories giving the value of liberty high priority, whereas other cultures will appear to be built around the priority ranking expressed by one of Brecht's characters: "Grub first; freedom later." If this is really all biological, all part of the evolved nature of the species, wouldn't we expect more uniformity than this?

14. *On Human Nature*, pp. 198–99.

15. "Each man would soon learn that if he aided his fellow-men, he would commonly receive aid in return. From this low motive he might acquire the habit of aiding his fellows" (*The Descent of Man*, Chap. V, p. 499).

16. *On Human Nature*, pp. 155–56.

17. I want to thank Cora Diamond for raising the worries that provoked the foregoing paragraph. In addition to the empirical and conceptual problems faced by Wilson's account, there are also, in my judgment, some nontrivial *moral* problems with it as well. Wilson, like Mill and other rule utilitarians, regards rights as only instrumentally valuable—i.e., he regards rights as domains worth protecting on grounds of the consequential value of so doing. But there is another tradition, the natural rights tradition, that sees rights as in a sense intrinsically valuable, as ways human beings have to express what is essential about their natures as free and rational choosers. This view of rights may be unsupportable, but it at least deserves consideration and reasoned rejection if it is to be rejected. See my "Rights and Borderline Cases" and other essays in my *Retribution, Justice and Therapy: Essays in the Philosophy of Law* (Dordrecht and Boston: D. Reidel, 1979).

18. *Supra* note 4, pp. 196–205.

19. *Ibid.*, p. 196.

20. *Ibid.*, pp 198, 204.

21. In his valuable article "Hopes, Fears, and Sociobiology" (forthcoming in *Queen's Quarterly*), my colleague John Beatty suggests that sociobiologists sometimes ignore two important distinctions that all of us in philosophy know how to make: (1) a distinction between reasons and causes, and (2) a related distinction between explaining why a belief is in fact held and justifying a belief that one ought to act in a certain way. There are standard distinctions we always draw for our students in introductory courses. But there is a very important sense in which *these are the very distinctions that sociobiology seeks to challenge!* Thus if one rejects sociobiology because it fails to draw these distinctions, then one is simply begging the question against it, and if one tries to "save" sociobiology by showing that its practitioners sometimes embrace those distinctions, then one is rendering sociobiology inane by failing to see the genuinely profound, exciting, and troubling issues it raises. The sociobiologist may well agree with the point (made by Beatty) that value judgments are properly defended in terms of other value judgments until we reach some that are fundamental. All of this, in a sense, is the giving of *reasons*. However, suppose we seriously raise the question of why these fundamental judgments are regarded as fundamental. There may be only a *causal* explanation for this! We reject simplistic utilitarianism because it entails consequences that are morally *counterintuitive*, or we embrace a Rawlsian theory of justice because it systematizes (places in "reflective equilibrium") our *pretheoretical convictions*. But what is the status of those intuitions or convictions? Perhaps there is nothing more to be said for them than that they involve deep *preferences* (or patterns of preference) built into our biological nature. If this is so, then at a very fundamental point the reasons/causes (and the belief we ought/really ought) distinction breaks down, or the one transforms into the other. This may all be wrong, of course, but it is at least interesting at a rather profound level, and it

requires something more by way of a response than attacking it with the very distinctions it seeks to undermine.

22. After I had completed the present book I came across Peter Singer's article "Ethics and Sociobiology" in *Philosophy and Public Affairs* 11, No. 1 (Winter, 1982): 40–64. I think the article is excellent and I highly recommend it to readers of the present volume. Singer suggests briefly (pp. 55–57) that one plausible way to construe sociobiology is as providing a basis for moral skepticism—a suggestion that obviously has my whole-hearted endorsement. Singer's article is adapted from his book *The Expanding Circle: Ethics and Sociobiology* (New York: Farrar, Straus & Giroux, 1981), a book I wish I had known of before writing my own.

23. I am currently doing research for a book on the right to privacy, wherein I shall have to examine the nature of privacy and consider why we tend to place such a high value on privacy. I have been sufficiently influenced by sociobiology that I now consider it essential to see what biological literature may contribute to our understanding of this value. It will not tell the whole story, surely, and it may contribute nothing at all, but I am persuaded it is worth a look, and I am glad to have my intellectual and moral horizons thus expanded.

Conclusion

In my opening chapter, I expressed the conviction that moral philosophy cannot be put upon the kind of secure foundation that some of its practitioners have hoped for; I also expressed the Humean conviction that in all practical matters this did not really matter very much. How we treat others and whether we regard ourselves as leading meaningful lives is deeply rooted in how we *feel*—something that never depended upon a theoretical foundation and thus will not disappear without it.

I am inclined to think that biology (our evolved passionate nature) may explain in part both the failure and why the failure does not matter. The failure is inevitable because at some crucial point our theories are grounded on how we feel—how we treat others being deeply rooted in how we feel; whether we regard ourselves as leading meaningful lives being deeply rooted in how we feel. We may call these feelings intuitions or pretheoretical convictions or even self-evident truths, but this does not stop them from being a part of our passionate and not our intellectual nature. They are the matter on which the intellect must operate—the real sense, by the way, of the famous Humean claim that reason is the slave of the passions. But since these feelings are more primitive than reason and constitute the framework in which reason itself must operate, they serve to keep us going even when the reasons run out. The fabric of our lives never ultimately depended upon theory, but rather upon the brute facts about us that theory, for all its pretensions to the contrary, simply organizes: our feelings, our desires, our instincts, our passions. To see ourselves in terms of these passions and their origins is to see ourselves in biological and evolutionary terms. This is not the only perspective on human life, surely, but on issues of ethics and the meaning of life it is one of the useful ones, particularly when we bump up against the question of what to do when the theories and reasons give out. This is a point at which many philosophers and theologians like to begin talking about commitment or leaps of faith—some process of accepting as proven that which in principle cannot be proven. I myself find it much more intellectually and personally clarifying to start talking here about biology instead.

APPENDIX A

McLean v. Arkansas Board of Education

On 5 January 1982 U.S. District Court Judge William R. Overton enjoined the Arkansas Board of Education from implementing the "Balanced Treatment for Creation-Science and Evolution-Science Act" of the state legislature. This is the complete text of his judgment, injunction, and opinion in the case.

Judgment

Pursuant to the Court's Memorandum Opinion filed this date, judgment is hereby entered in favor of the plaintiffs and against the defendants. The relief prayed for is granted.

Dated this January 5, 1982.

Injunction

Pursuant to the Court's Memorandum Opinion filed this date, the defendants and each of them and all their servants and employees are hereby permanently enjoined from implementing in any manner Act 590 of the Acts of Arkansas of 1981.

It is so ordered this January 5, 1982.

Memorandum Opinion

Introduction

On March 19, 1981, the Governor of Arkansas signed into law Act 590 of 1981, entitled the "Balanced Treatment for Creation-Science and Evolution-Science Act." The Act is codified as Ark. Stat. Ann. §80–1663, *et seq.*, (1981 Supp.). Its essential mandate is stated in its first sentence: "Public schools within this State shall give balanced treatment to creation-science and to evolution-science." On May 27, 1981, this suit was filed *(1)* challenging the constitutional validity of Act 590 on three distinct grounds.

First, it is contended that Act 590 constitutes an establishment of religion prohibited by the First Amendment to the Constitution, which is made applicable to the states by the Fourteenth Amendment. Second, the plaintiffs argue the Act violates a right to academic freedom which they say is guaranteed to students and teachers by the Free Speech Clause of the First Amendment. Third, plaintiffs allege the Act is impermissibly vague and thereby violates the Due Process Clause of the Fourteenth Amendment.

The individual plaintiffs include the resident Arkansas Bishops of the United Methodist, Episcopal, Roman Catholic and African Methodist Episcopal Churches, the principal official of the Presbyterian Churches in Arkansas, other United Methodist, Southern Baptist and Presbyterian clergy, as well as several persons who sue as parents and next friends of minor children attending Arkansas public schools. One plaintiff is a high school biology teacher. All are also Arkansas taxpayers. Among the organizational plaintiffs are the American Jewish Congress, the Union of American Hebrew Congregations, the American Jewish Committee, the Arkansas Education Association, the National Association of Biology Teachers and the National Coalition for Public Education and Religious Liberty, all of which sue on behalf of members living in Arkansas *(2)*.

The defendants include the Arkansas Board of Education and its members, the Director of the Department of Education, and the State Textbooks and Instructional Materials Selecting Committee *(3)*. The Pulaski County Special School District and its Directors and Superintendent were voluntarily dismissed by the plaintiffs at the pre-trial conference held October 1, 1981.

The trial commenced December 7, 1981, and continued through December 17, 1981. This Memorandum Opinion constitutes the Court's findings of fact and conclusions of law. Further orders and judgment will be in conformity with this opinion.

I

There is no controversy over the legal standards under which the Establishment Clause portion of this case must be judged. The Supreme Court has on a number of occasions expounded on the meaning of the clause, and the pronouncements are clear. Often the issue has arisen in the context of public education, as it has here. In *Everson v. Board of Education*, 330 U.S. 1, 15–16 (1947), Justice Black stated:

The "establishment of religion" clause of the First Amendment means at least this: Neither a state nor the Federal Government can set up a church. Neither can pass laws which aid one religion, aid all religions, or prefer one religion over another. Neither can force nor influence a person to go to or to remain away from church against his will or force him to profess a belief or disbelief in any religion. No person can be punished for entertaining or professing religious beliefs or disbeliefs, for church-attendance or non-attendance. No tax, large or small, can be levied to support any religious activities or institutions, whatever they may be called, or whatever form they may adopt to teach or practice religion. Neither a state nor the Federal Government can, openly or secretly, participate in the affairs of any religious organizations or groups and *vice versa*. In the words of Jefferson, the clause . . . was intended to erect "a wall of separation between church and State."

The Establishment Clause thus enshrines two central values: voluntarism and pluralism. And it is in the area of the public schools that these values must be guarded most vigilantly.

Designed to serve as perhaps the most powerful agency for promoting cohesion among a heterogeneous democratic people, the public school must keep scrupulously free from entanglement in the strife of sects. The preservation of the community from divisive conflicts, of Government from irreconcilable pressures by religious groups, of religion from censorship and coercion however subtly exercised, requires strict confinement of the State to instruction other than religious, leaving to the individual's church and home, indoctrination in the faith of his choice. [*McCollum v.*

Board of Education, 333 U.S. 203, 216–217 (1948), (Opinion of Frankfurter, J., joined by Jackson, Burton and Rutledge, J. J.)]

The specific formulation of the establishment prohibition has been refined over the years, but its meaning has not varied from the principles articulated by Justice Black in *Everson*. In *Abbington School District v. Schempp*, 374 U.S. 203, 222 (1963), Justice Clark stated that "to withstand the strictures of the Establishment Clause there must be a secular legislative purpose and a primary effect that neither advances nor inhibits religion." The Court found it quite clear that the First Amendment does not permit a state to require the daily reading of the Bible in public schools, for "[s]urely the place of the Bible as an instrument of religion cannot be gainsaid." *Id.* at 224. Similarly, in *Engel v. Vitale*, 370 U.S. 421 (1962), the Court held that the First Amendment prohibited the New York Board of Regents from requiring the daily recitation of a certain prayer in the schools. With characteristic succinctness, Justice Black wrote, "Under [the First] Amendment's prohibition against governmental establishment of religion, as reinforced by the provisions of the Fourteenth Amendment, government in this country, be it state or federal, is without power to prescribe by law any particular form of prayer which is to be used as an official prayer in carrying on any program of governmentally sponsored religious activity." *Id.* at 430. Black also identified the objective at which the Establishment Clause was aimed: "Its first and most immediate purpose rested on the belief that a union of government and religion tends to destroy government and to degrade religion." *Id.* at 431.

Most recently, the Supreme Court has held that the clause prohibits a state from requiring the posting of the Ten Commandments in public school classrooms for the same reasons that officially imposed daily Bible reading is prohibited. *Stone v. Graham*, 449 U.S. 39 (1980). The opinion in *Stone* relies on the most recent formulation of the Establishment Clause test, that of *Lemon v. Kurtzman*, 403 U.S. 602, 612–613 (1971):

First, the statute must have a secular legislative purpose; second, its principal or primary effect must be one that neither advances nor inhibits religion . . .; finally, the statute must not foster "an excessive government entanglement with religion." [*Stone v. Graham*, 449 U.S. at 40]

It is under this three part test that the evidence in this case must be judged. Failure on any of these grounds is fatal to the enactment.

II

The religious movement known as Fundamentalism began in nineteenth century America as part of evangelical Protestantism's response to social changes, new religious thought and Darwinism. Fundamentalists viewed these developments as attacks on the Bible and as responsible for a decline in traditional values.

The various manifestations of Fundamentalism have had a number of common characteristics (4), but a central premise has always been a literal interpretation of the Bible and a belief in the inerrancy of the Scriptures. Following World War I, there was again a perceived decline in traditional morality, and Fundamentalism focused on evolution as responsible for the decline. One aspect of their efforts, particularly in the South, was the promotion of statutes prohibiting the teaching of evolution in public schools. In Arkansas, this resulted in the adoption of Initiated Act 1 of 1929 (5).

Between the 1920's and early 1960's, anti-evolutionary sentiment had a subtle but pervasive influence on the teaching of biology in public schools. Generally, textbooks avoided the topic of evolution and did not mention the name of Darwin. Following the launch of the Sputnik satellite by the Soviet Union in 1957, the National Science Foundation funded several programs designed to modernize the teaching of science in the nation's schools. The Biological Sciences Curriculum Study (BSCS), a nonprofit organization, was among those receiving grants for curriculum study and revision. Working with scientists and teachers, BSCS developed a series of biology texts which, although emphasizing different aspects of biology, incorporated the theory of evolution as a major theme. The success of the BSCS effort is shown by the fact that fifty percent of American school children currently use BSCS books directly and the curriculum is incorporated indirectly in virtually all biology texts. (Testimony of Mayer; Nelkin, Px 1) (6).

In the early 1960's, there was again a resurgence of concern among Fundamentalists about the loss of traditional values and a fear of growing secularism in society. The Fundamentalist movement became more active and has steadily grown in numbers and political influence. There is an emphasis among current Fundamentalists on the literal interpretation of the Bible and the Book of Genesis as the sole source of knowledge about origins.

The term "scientific creationism" first gained currency around 1965 following publication of *The Genesis Flood* in 1961 by Whitcomb and Morris. There is undoubtedly some connection between the appearance of the BSCS texts emphasizing evolutionary thought and efforts by Fundamentalists to attack the theory. (Mayer)

In the 1960's and early 1970's, several Fundamentalist organizations were formed to promote the idea that the Book of Genesis was supported by scientific data. The terms "creation science" and "scientific creationism" have been adopted by these Fundamentalists as descriptive of their study of creation and the origins of man. Perhaps the leading creationist organization is the Institute for Creation Research (ICR), which is affiliated with the Christian Heritage College and supported by the Scott Memorial Baptist Church in San Diego, California. The ICR, through the Creation-Life Publishing Company, is the leading publisher of creation science material. Other creation science organizations include the Creation Science Research Center (CSRC) of San Diego and the Bible Science Association of Minneapolis, Minnesota. In 1963, the Creation Research Society (CRS) was formed from a schism in the American Scientific Affiliation (ASA). It is an organization of literal Fundamentalists (7) who have the equivalent of a master's degree in some recognized area of science. A purpose of the organization is "to reach all people with the vital message of the scientific and historic truth about creation." Nelkin, *The Science Textbook Controversies and the Politics of Equal Time*, 66. Similarly, the CSRC was formed in 1970 from a split in the CRS. Its aim has been "to reach the 63 million children of the United States with the scientific teaching of Biblical creationism." *Id.* at 69.

Among creationist writers who are recognized as authorities in the field by other creationists are Henry M. Morris, Duane Gish, G. E. Parker, Harold S. Slusher, Richard B. Bliss, John W. Moore, Martin E. Clark, W. L. Wysong, Robert E. Kofahl and Kelly L. Segraves. Morris is Director of ICR, Gish is Associate Director and Segraves is associated with CSRC.

Creationists view evolution as a source of society's ills, and the writings of Morris and Clark are typical expressions of that view.

Evolution is thus not only anti-Biblical and anti-Christian, but it is utterly unscientific and impossible as well. But it has served effectively as the pseudo-scientific basis of atheism, agnosticism, socialism, fascism, and numerous other false and dangerous philosophies over the past century. [Morris and Clark, *The Bible Has The Answer*, (Px 31 and Pretrial Px 89) *(8)*]

Creationists have adopted the view of Fundamentalists generally that there are only two positions with respect to the origins of the earth and life: belief in the inerrancy of the Genesis story of creation and of a worldwide flood as fact, or belief in what they call evolution.

Henry Morris has stated, "It is impossible to devise a legitimate means of harmonizing the Bible with evolution." Morris, "Evolution and the Bible," *ICR Impact Series* Number 5 (undated, unpaged), quoted in Mayer, Px 8, at 3. This dualistic approach to the subject of origins permeates the creationist literature.

The creationist organizations consider the introduction of creation science into the public schools part of their ministry. The ICR has published at least two pamphlets *(9)* containing suggested methods for convincing school boards, administrators and teachers that creationism should be taught in public schools. The ICR has urged its proponents to encourage school officials to voluntarily add creationism to the curriculum *(10)*.

Citizens For Fairness In Education is an organization based in Anderson, South Carolina, formed by Paul Ellwanger, a respiratory therapist who is trained in neither law nor science. Mr. Ellwanger is of the opinion that evolution is the forerunner of many social ills, including Nazism, racism, and abortion. (Ellwanger Depo. at 32–34). About 1977, Ellwanger collected several proposed legislative acts with the idea of preparing a model state act requiring the teaching of creationism as science in opposition to evolution. One of the proposals he collected was prepared by Wendell Bird, who is now a staff attorney for ICR *(11)*. From these various proposals, Ellwanger prepared a "model act" which calls for "balanced treatment" of "scientific creationism" and "evolution" in public schools. He circulated the proposed act to various people and organizations around the country.

Mr. Ellwanger's views on the nature of creation science are entitled to some weight since he personally drafted the model act which became Act 590. His evidentiary deposition with exhibits and unnumbered attachments (produced in response to a subpoena *duces tecum*) speaks to both the intent of the Act and the scientific merits of creation science. Mr. Ellwanger does not believe creation science is a science. In a letter to Pastor Robert E. Hays he states, "While neither evolution nor creation can qualify as a scientific theory, and since it is virtually impossible at this point to educate the whole world that evolution is not a true scientific theory, we have freely used these terms—the evolution theory and the theory of scientific creationism—in the bill's text." (Unnumbered attachment to Ellwanger Depo., at 2.) He further states in a letter to Mr. Tom Bethell, "As we examine evolution (remember, we're not making any scientific claims for creation, but we are challenging evolution's claim to be scientific) . . ." (Unnumbered attachment to Ellwanger Depo. at 1.)

Ellwanger's correspondence on the subject shows an awareness that Act 590 is a religious crusade, coupled with a desire to conceal this fact. In a letter to State Senator Bill Keith of Louisiana, he says, "I view this whole battle as one between God and anti-God forces, though I know there are a large number of evolutionists who believe in God." And further, ". . . it behooves Satan to do all he can to thwart our efforts and confuse the issue at every turn." Yet Ellwanger suggests to Senator Keith, "If you have a clear choice between having grassroots leaders of this statewide bill promotion effort to be ministerial or non-ministerial, be sure to opt for the non-ministerial. It does the bill effort no good to have ministers out there in the public forum and the adversary will surely pick at this point. . . . Ministerial persons can accomplish a tremendous amount of work from behind the scenes, encouraging their congregations to take the organizational and P.R. initiatives. And they can lead their churches in storming Heaven with prayers for help against so tenacious an adversary." (Unnumbered attachment to Ellwanger Depo. at 1.)

Ellwanger shows a remarkable degree of political candor, if not finesse, in a letter to State Senator Joseph Carlucci of Florida:

2. It would be very wise, if not actually essential, that all of us who are engaged in this legislative effort be careful not to present our position and

our work in a religious framework. For example, in written communications that might somehow be shared with those other persons whom we may be trying to convince, it would be well to exclude our own personal testimony and/or witness for Christ, but rather, if we are so moved, to give that testimony on a separate attached note. (Unnumbered attachment to Ellwanger Depo. at 1.)

The same tenor is reflected in a letter by Ellwanger to Mary Ann Miller, a member of FLAG (Family, Life, America under God) who lobbied the Arkansas Legislature in favor of Act 590:

. . . we'd like to suggest that you and your co-workers be very cautious about mixing creation-science with creation-religion . . . Please urge your co-workers not to allow themselves to get sucked into the "religion" trap of mixing the two together, for such mixing does incalculable harm to the legislative thrust. It could even bring public opinion to bear adversely upon the higher courts that will eventually have to pass judgment on the constitutionality of this new law. (Ex. 1 to Miller Depo.)

Perhaps most interesting, however, is Mr. Ellwanger's testimony in his deposition as to his strategy for having the model act implemented:

Q.   You're trying to play on other people's religious motives.
A.   I'm trying to play on their emotions, love, hate, their likes, dislikes, because I don't know any other way to involve, to get humans to become involved in human endeavors. I see emotions as being a healthy and legitimate means of getting people's feelings into action, and . . . I believe that the predominance of population in America that represents the greatest potential for taking some kind of action in this area is a Christian community. I see the Jewish community as far less potential in taking action . . . but I've seen a lot of interest among Christians and I feel, why not exploit that to get the bill going if that's what it takes. (Ellwanger Depo. at 146–147.)

Mr. Ellwanger's ultimate purpose is revealed in the closing of his letter to Mr. Tom Bethell: "Perhaps all this is old hat to you, Tom, and if so, I'd appreciate your telling me so and perhaps where you've heard it before—the idea of killing evolution instead of playing these debating games that we've been playing for nigh over a decade already." (Unnumbered attachment to Ellwanger Depo. at 3.)

It was out of this milieu that Act 590 emerged. The Reverend W. A. Blount, a Biblical literalist who is pastor of a church in the Little Rock area and was, in February, 1981, chairman of the Greater Little Rock Evangelical Fellowship, was among those who received a copy of the model act from Ellwanger (12).

At Reverend Blount's request, the Evangelical Fellowship unanimously adopted a resolution to seek introduction of Ellwanger's act in the Arkansas Legislature. A committee composed of two ministers, Curtis Thomas and W. A. Young, was appointed to implement the resolution. Thomas obtained from Ellwanger a revised copy of the model act which he transmitted to Carl Hunt, a business associate of Senator James L. Holsted, with the request that Hunt prevail upon Holsted to introduce the act.

Holsted, a self-described "born again" Christian Fundamentalist, introduced the act in the Arkansas Senate. He did not consult the State Department of Education, scientists, science educators or the Arkansas Attorney General (13). The Act was not referred to any Senate committee for hearing and was passed after only a few minutes' discussion on the Senate floor. In the House of Representatives, the bill was referred to the Education Committee which conducted a perfunctory fifteen minute hearing. No scientist testified at the hearing, nor was any representative from the State Department of Education called to testify.

Ellwanger's model act was enacted into law in Arkansas as Act 590 without amendment or modification other than minor typographical changes. The legislative "findings of fact" in Ellwanger's act and Act 590 are identical, although no meaningful fact-finding process was employed by the General Assembly.

Ellwanger's efforts in preparation of the model act and campaign for its adoption in the states were motivated by his opposition to the theory of evolution and his desire to see the Biblical version of creation taught in the public schools. There is no evidence that the pastors, Blount, Thomas, Young or The Greater Little Rock Evangelical Fellowship were motivated by anything other than their religious convictions when proposing its adoption or during their lobbying efforts in its behalf. Senator Holsted's sponsorship and lobbying efforts in behalf of the Act were motivated solely by his religious beliefs and desire to see the Biblical version of creation taught in the public schools (14).

The State of Arkansas, like a number of states whose citizens have relatively homogeneous religious beliefs, has a long history of official opposition to evolution which is motivated by adherence to Fundamentalist beliefs in the inerrancy of the Book of Genesis. This history is documented in Justice Fortas' opinion in *Epperson v. Arkansas*, 393 U.S. 97 (1968), which struck down Initiated Act 1 of 1929, Ark. Stat. Ann. §§80–1627–1628, prohibiting the teaching of the theory of evolution. To this same tradition may be attributed Initiated Act 1 of 1930, Ark. Stat. Ann. §80–1606 (Repl. 1980), requiring "the reverent daily reading of a portion of the English Bible" in every public school classroom in the State *(15)*.

It is true, as defendants argue, that courts should look to legislative statements of a statute's purpose in Establishment Clause cases and accord such pronouncements great deference. See, e.g., *Committee for Public Education & Religious Liberty v. Nyquist*, 413 U.S. 756, 773 (1973) and *McGowan v. Maryland*, 366 U.S. 420, 445 (1961). Defendants also correctly state the principle that remarks by the sponsor or author of a bill are not considered controlling in analyzing legislative intent. See, e.g., *United States v. Emmons*, 410 U.S. 396 (1973) and *Chrysler Corp. v. Brown*, 441 U.S. 281 (1979).

Courts are not bound, however, by legislative statements of purpose or legislative disclaimers. *Stone v. Graham*, 449 U.S. 39 (1980); *Abbington School Dist. v. Schempp*, 374 U.S. 203 (1963). In determining the legislative purpose of a statute, courts may consider evidence of the historical context of the Act, *Epperson v. Arkansas*, 393 U.S. 97 (1968), the specific sequence of events leading up to passage of the Act, departures from normal procedural sequences, substantive departures from the normal, *Village of Arlington Heights v. Metropolitan Housing Corp.*, 429 U.S. 252 (1977), and contemporaneous statements of the legislative sponsor, *Fed. Energy Admin. v. Algonquin SNG, Inc.*, 426 U.S. 548, 564 (1976).

The unusual circumstances surrounding the passage of Act 590, as well as the substantive law of the First Amendment, warrant an inquiry into the stated legislative purposes. The author of the Act had publicly proclaimed the sectarian purpose of the proposal. The Arkansas residents who sought legislative sponsorship of the bill did so for a purely sectarian purpose. These circumstances alone may not be particularly persuasive, but when considered with the

publicly announced motives of the legislative sponsor made contemporaneously with the legislative process; the lack of any legislative investigation, debate or consultation with any educators or
scientists; the unprecedented intrusion in school curriculum (16);
and official history of the State of Arkansas on the subject, it is
obvious that the statement of purposes has little, if any, support in
fact. The state failed to produce any evidence which would warrant
an inference or conclusion that at any point in the process anyone
considered the legitimate educational value of the Act. It was
simply and purely an effort to introduce the Biblical version of
creation into the public school curricula. The only inference which
can be drawn from these circumstances is that the Act was passed
with the specific purpose by the General Assembly of advancing
religion. The Act therefore fails the first prong of the three-pronged
test, that of secular legislative purpose, as articulated in *Lemon v.
Kurtzman, supra,* and *Stone v. Graham, supra.*

III

If the defendants are correct and the Court is limited to an
examination of the language of the Act, the evidence is overwhelming that both the purpose and effect of Act 590 is the
advancement of religion in the public schools.

Section 4 of the Act provides:

Definitions, as used in this Act:

(a) "Creation-science" means the scientific evidences for creation and
inferences from those scientific evidences. Creation-science includes the
scientific evidences and related inferences that indicate: (1) Sudden creation of the universe, energy, and life from nothing; (2) The insufficiency of
mutation and natural selection in bringing about development of all living
kinds from a single organism; (3) Changes only within fixed limits of
originally created kinds of plants and animals; (4) Separate ancestry for
man and apes; (5) Explanation of the earth's geology by catastrophism,
including the occurrence of a worldwide flood; and (6) A relatively recent
inception of the earth and living kinds.

(b) "Evolution-science" means the scientific evidences for evolution and
inferences from those scientific evidences. Evolution-science includes the
scientific evidences and related inferences that indicate: (1) Emergence by
naturalistic processes of the universe from disordered matter and emer-

gence of life from nonlife; (2) The sufficiency of mutation and natural selection in bringing about development of present living kinds from simple earlier kinds; (3) Emergence by mutation and natural selection of present living kinds from simple earlier kinds; (4) Emergence of man from a common ancestor with apes; (5) Explanation of the earth's geology and the evolutionary sequence by uniformitarianism; and (6) An inception several billion years ago of the earth and somewhat later of life.

(c) "Public schools" mean public secondary and elementary schools.

The evidence establishes that the definition of "creation science" contained in 4(a) has as its unmentioned reference the first 11 chapters of the Book of Genesis. Among the many creation epics in human history, the account of sudden creation from nothing, or *creatio ex nihilo*, and subsequent destruction of the world by flood is unique to Genesis. The concepts of 4(a) are the literal Fundamentalists' view of Genesis. Section 4(a) is unquestionably a statement of religion, with the exception of 4(a)(2) which is a negative thrust aimed at what the creationists understand to be the theory of evolution *(17)*.

Both the concepts and wording of Section 4(a) convey an inescapable religiosity. Section 4(a)(1) describes "sudden creation of the universe, energy and life from nothing." Every theologian who testified, including defense witnesses, expressed the opinion that the statement referred to a supernatural creation which was performed by God.

Defendants argue that: (1) the fact that 4(a) conveys ideas similar to the literal interpretation of Genesis does not make it conclusively a statement of religion; (2) that reference to a creation from nothing is not necessarily a religious concept since the Act only suggests a creator who has power, intelligence and a sense of design and not necessarily the attributes of love, compassion and justice *(18)*; and (3) that simply teaching about the concept of a creator is not a religious exercise unless the student is required to make a commitment to the concept of a creator.

The evidence fully answers these arguments. The ideas of 4(a)(1) are not merely similar to the literal interpretation of Genesis; they are identical and parallel to no other story of creation *(19)*.

The argument that creation from nothing in 4(a)(1) does not involve a supernatural deity has no evidentiary or rational support. To the contrary, "creation out of nothing" is a concept unique to Western religions. In traditional Western religious thought, the conception of a creator of the world is a conception of God. Indeed, creation of the world "out of nothing" is the ultimate religious statement because God is the only actor. As Dr. Langdon Gilkey noted, the Act refers to one who has the power to bring all the universe into existence from nothing. The only "one" who has this power is God (20).

The leading creationist writers, Morris and Gish, acknowledge that the idea of creation described in 4(a)(1) is the concept of creation by God and make no pretense to the contrary (21). The idea of sudden creation from nothing, or *creatio ex nihilo*, is an inherently religious concept. (Vawter, Gilkey, Geisler, Ayala, Blount, Hicks.)

The argument advanced by defendants' witness, Dr. Norman Geisler, that teaching the existence of God is not religious unless the teaching seeks a commitment, is contrary to common understanding and contradicts settled case law. *Stone v. Graham*, 449 U.S. 39 (1980); *Abbington School District v. Schempp*, 374 U.S. 203 (1963).

The facts that creation science is inspired by the Book of Genesis and that Section 4(a) is consistent with a literal interpretation of Genesis leave no doubt that a major effect of the Act is the advancement of particular religious beliefs. The legal impact of this conclusion will be discussed further at the conclusion of the Court's evaluation of the scientific merit of creation science.

IV(A)

The approach to teaching "creation science" and "evolution science" found in Act 590 is identical to the two-model approach espoused by the Institute for Creation Research and is taken almost verbatim from ICR writings. It is an extension of Fundamentalists' view that one must either accept the literal interpretation of Genesis or else believe in the godless system of evolution.

The two model approach of the creationists is simply a contrived dualism (22) which has no scientific factual basis or legitimate educational purpose. It assumes only two explanations for the origins of life and existence of man, plants and animals: It was either the work of a creator or it was not. Application of these two models, according to creationists, and the defendants, dictates that all scientific evidence which fails to support the theory of evolution is necessarily scientific evidence in support of creationism and is, therefore, creation science "evidence" in support of Section 4(a).

IV(B)

The emphasis on origins as an aspect of the theory of evolution is peculiar to creationist literature. Although the subject of origins of life is within the province of biology, the scientific community does not consider origins of life a part of evolutionary theory. The theory of evolution assumes the existence of life and is directed to an explanation of *how* life evolved. Evolution does not presuppose the absence of a creator or God and the plain inference conveyed by Section 4 is erroneous *(23)*.

As a statement of the theory of evolution, Section 4(b) is simply a hodgepodge of limited assertions, many of which are factually inaccurate.

For example, although 4(b)(2) asserts, as a tenet of evolutionary theory, "the sufficiency of mutation and natural selection in bringing about the existence of present living kinds from simple earlier kinds," Drs. Ayala and Gould both stated that biologists know that these two processes do not account for all significant evolutionary change. They testified to such phenomena as recombination, the founder effect, genetic drift and the theory of punctuated equilibrium, which are believed to play important evolutionary roles. Section 4(b) omits any reference to these. Moreover, 4(b) utilizes the term "kinds" which all scientists said is not a word of science and has no fixed meaning. Additionally, the Act presents both evolution and creation science as "package deals." Thus, evidence critical of some aspect of what the creationists define as evolution is taken as support for a theory which includes a worldwide flood and a relatively young earth *(24)*.

IV(C)

In addition to the fallacious pedagogy of the two model approach, Section 4(a) lacks legitimate educational value because "creation science" as defined in that section is simply not science. Several witnesses suggested definitions of science. A descriptive definition was said to be that science is what is "accepted by the scientific community" and is "what scientists do." The obvious implication of this description is that, in a free society, knowledge does not require the imprimatur of legislation in order to become science.

More precisely, the essential characteristics of science are:

(1) It is guided by natural law;

(2) It has to be explanatory by reference to natural law;

(3) It is testable against the empirical world;

(4) Its conclusions are tentative, i.e., are not necessarily the final word; and

(5) It is falsifiable. (Ruse and other science witnesses).

Creation science as described in Section 4(a) fails to meet these essential characteristics. First, the section revolves around 4(a)(1) which asserts a sudden creation "from nothing." Such a concept is not science because it depends upon a supernatural intervention which is not guided by natural law. It is not explanatory by reference to natural law, is not testable and is not falsifiable (25).

If the unifying idea of supernatural creation by God is removed from Section 4, the remaining parts of the section explain nothing and are meaningless assertions.

Section 4(a)(2), relating to the "insufficiency of mutation and natural selection in bringing about development of all living kinds from a single organism," is an incomplete negative generalization directed at the theory of evolution.

Section 4(a)(3) which describes "changes only within fixed limits of originally created kinds of plants and animals" fails to conform to the essential characteristics of science for several reasons. First, there is no scientific definition of "kinds" and none of the witnesses was able to point to any scientific authority which recognized the term or knew how many "kinds" existed. One defense witness suggested there may be 100 to 10,000 different "kinds." Another believes there were "about 10,000, give or take a few thousand." Second, the assertion appears to be an effort to establish outer limits of changes within species. There is no scientific explanation for these limits which is guided by natural law and the limitations, whatever they are, cannot be explained by natural law.

The statement in 4(a)(4) of "separate ancestry of man and apes" is a bald assertion. It explains nothing and refers to no scientific fact or theory (26).

Section 4(a)(5) refers to "explanation of the earth's geology by catastrophism, including the occurrence of a worldwide flood." This assertion completely fails as science. The Act is referring to the Noachian flood described in the Book of Genesis (27). The creationist writers concede that *any* kind of Genesis Flood depends upon supernatural intervention. A worldwide flood as an explanation of the world's geology is not the product of natural law, nor can its occurrence be explained by natural law.

Section 4(a)(6) equally fails to meet the standards of science. "Relatively recent inception" has no scientific meaning. It can only be given meaning by reference to creationist writings which place the age at between 6,000 and 20,000 years because of the genealogy of the Old Testament. See, e.g., Px 78, Gish (6,000 to 10,000); Px 87, Segraves (6,000 to 20,000). Such a reasoning process is not the product of natural law; not explainable by natural law; nor is it tentative.

Creation science, as defined in Section 4(a), not only fails to follow the canons defining scientific theory, it also fails to fit the more general descriptions of "what scientists think" and "what scientists do." The scientific community consists of individuals and groups, nationally and internationally, who work independently in such varied fields as biology, paleontology, geology and astronomy. Their work is published and subject to review and testing by their peers. The journals for publication are both numerous and varied. There is, however, not one recognized scientific journal which has published an article espousing the creation science theory described in Section 4(a). Some of the State's witnesses suggested that the scientific community was "close-minded" on the subject of creationism and that explained the lack of acceptance of the creation science arguments. Yet no witness produced a scientific article for which publication had been refused. Perhaps some members of the scientific community are resistant to new ideas. It is, however, inconceivable that such a loose knit group of independent thinkers in all the varied fields of science could, or would, so effectively censor new scientific thought.

The creationists have difficulty maintaining among their ranks consistency in the claim that creationism is science. The author of Act 590, Ellwanger, said that neither evolution nor creationism was science. He thinks both are religion. Duane Gish recently responded to an article in *Discover* critical of creationism by stating:

Stephen Jay Gould states that creationists claim creation is a scientific theory. This is a false accusation. Creationists have repeatedly stated that neither creation nor evolution is a scientific theory (and each is equally religious). (Gish, letter to editor of *Discover*, July, 1981, App. 30 to Plaintiffs' Pretrial Brief)

The methodology employed by creationists is another factor which is indicative that their work is not science. A scientific theory must be tentative and always subject to revision or abandonment in light of facts that are inconsistent with, or falsify, the theory. A theory that is by its own terms dogmatic, absolutist and never subject to revision is not a scientific theory.

The creationists' methods do not take data, weigh it against the opposing scientific data, and thereafter reach the conclusions stated in Section 4(a). Instead, they take the literal wording of the Book of Genesis and attempt to find scientific support for it. The method is best explained in the language of Morris in his book (Px 31) *Studies in The Bible and Science* at page 114:

. . . it is . . . quite impossible to determine anything about Creation through a study of present processes, because present processes are not creative in character. If man wishes to know anything about Creation (the time of Creation, the duration of Creation, the order of Creation, the methods of Creation, or anything else) his sole source of true information is that of divine revelation. God was there when it happened. We were not there. . . . Therefore, we are completely limited to what God has seen fit to tell us, and this information is in His written Word. This is our textbook on the science of Creation!

The Creation Research Society employs the same unscientific approach to the issue of creationism. Its applicants for membership must subscribe to the belief that the Book of Genesis is "historically and scientifically true in all of the original autographs" (28). The Court would never criticize or discredit any person's testimony based on his or her religious beliefs. While anybody is free to approach a scientific inquiry in any fashion they choose, they cannot properly describe the methodology used as scientific, if they start with a conclusion and refuse to change it regardless of the evidence developed during the course of the investigation.

IV(D)

In efforts to establish "evidence" in support of creation science, the defendants relied upon the same false premise as the two model approach contained in Section 4, i.e., all evidence which criticized evolutionary theory was proof in support of creation science. For example, the defendants established that the mathematical probability of a chance chemical combination resulting in life from non-life is so remote that such an occurrence is almost beyond imagination. Those mathematical facts, the defendants argue, are scientific evidences that life was the product of a creator. While the statistical figures may be impressive evidence against the theory of chance chemical combinations as an explanation of origins, it requires a leap of faith to interpret those figures so as to support a complex doctrine which includes a sudden creation from nothing, a worldwide flood, separate ancestry of man and apes, and a young earth.

The defendants' argument would be more persuasive if, in fact, there were only two theories or ideas about the origins of life and the world. That there are a number of theories was acknowledged by the State's witnesses, Dr. Wickramasinghe and Dr. Geisler. Dr. Wickramasinghe testified at length in support of a theory that life on earth was "seeded" by comets which delivered genetic material and perhaps organisms to the earth's surface from interstellar dust far outside the solar system. The "seeding" theory further hypothesizes that the earth remains under the continuing influence of genetic material from space which continues to affect life. While Wickramasinghe's theory (29) about the origins of life on earth has not received general acceptance within the scientific community, he has, at least, used scientific methodology to produce a theory of origins which meets the essential characteristics of science.

The Court is at a loss to understand why Dr. Wickramasinghe was called in behalf of the defendants. Perhaps it was because he was generally critical of the theory of evolution and the scientific community, a tactic consistent with the strategy of the defense. Unfortunately for the defense, he demonstrated that the simplistic approach of the two model analysis of the origins of life is false. Furthermore, he corroborated the plaintiffs' witnesses by concluding that "no rational scientist" would believe the earth's geology could be explained by reference to a worldwide flood or that the earth was less than one million years old.

The proof in support of creation science consisted almost entirely of efforts to discredit the theory of evolution through a rehash of data and theories which have been before the scientific community for decades. The arguments asserted by creationists are not based upon new scientific evidence or laboratory data which has been ignored by the scientific community.

Robert Gentry's discovery of radioactive polonium haloes in granite and coalified woods is, perhaps, the most recent scientific work which the creationists use as argument for a "relatively recent inception" of the earth and a "worldwide flood." The existence of polonium haloes in granite and coalified wood is thought to be inconsistent with radiometric dating methods based upon constant radioactive decay rates. Mr. Gentry's findings were published almost ten years ago and have been the subject of some discussion in the scientific community. The discoveries have not, however, led to the formulation of any scientific hypothesis or theory which would explain a relatively recent inception of the earth or a worldwide flood. Gentry's discovery has been treated as a minor mystery which will eventually be explained. It may deserve further investigation, but the National Science Foundation has not deemed it to be of sufficient import to support further funding.

The testimony of Marianne Wilson was persuasive evidence that creation science is not science. Ms. Wilson is in charge of the science curriculum for Pulaski County Special School District, the largest school district in the State of Arkansas. Prior to the passage of Act 590, Larry Fisher, a science teacher in the District, using materials from the ICR, convinced the School Board that it should voluntarily adopt creation science as part of its science curriculum. The District Superintendent assigned Ms. Wilson the job of producing a creation science curriculum guide. Ms. Wilson's testimony about the project was particularly convincing because she obviously approached the assignment with an open mind and no preconceived notions about the subject. She had not heard of creation science until about a year ago and did not know its meaning before she began her research.

Ms. Wilson worked with a committee of science teachers appointed from the District. They reviewed practically all of the creationist literature. Ms. Wilson and the committee members reached the unanimous conclusion that creationism is not science; it is religion. They so reported to the Board. The Board ignored the recommendation and insisted that a curriculum guide be prepared.

In researching the subject, Ms. Wilson sought the assistance of Mr. Fisher who initiated the Board action and asked professors in the science departments of the University of Arkansas at Little Rock and the University of Central Arkansas (30) for reference material and assistance, and attended a workshop conducted at Central Baptist College by Dr. Richard Bliss of the ICR staff. Act 590 became law during the course of her work so she used Section 4(a) as a format for her curriculum guide.

Ms. Wilson found all available creationists' materials unacceptable because they were permeated with religious references and reliance upon religious beliefs.

It is easy to understand why Ms. Wilson and other educators find the creationists' textbook material and teaching guides unacceptable. The materials misstate the theory of evolution in the same fashion as Section 4(b) of the Act, with emphasis on the alternative mutually exclusive nature of creationism and evolution. Students are constantly encouraged to compare and make a choice between the two models, and the material is not presented in an accurate manner.

A typical example is *Origins* (Px 76) by Richard B. Bliss, Director of Curriculum Development of the ICR. The presentation begins with a chart describing "preconceived ideas about origins" which suggests that some people believe that evolution is atheistic. Concepts of evolution, such as "adaptive radiation" are erroneously presented. At page 11, figure 1.6, of the text, a chart purports to illustrate this "very important" part of the evolution model. The chart conveys the idea that such diverse mammals as a whale, bear, bat and monkey all evolved from a shrew through the process of adaptive radiation. Such a suggestion is, of course, a totally erroneous and misleading application of the theory. Even more objectionable, especially when viewed in light of the emphasis on asking the student to elect one of the models, is the chart presentation at page 17, figure 1.6. That chart purports to illustrate the evolutionists' belief that man evolved from bacteria to fish to reptile to mammals and, thereafter, into man. The illustration indicates, however, that the mammal from which man evolved was *a rat*.

Biology, A Search for Order in Complexity (31) is a high school biology text typical of creationists' materials. The following quotations are illustrative:

Flowers and roots do not have a mind to have purpose of their own; therefore, this planning must have been done for them by the Creator. (at page 12)

The exquisite beauty of color and shape in flowers exceeds the skill of poet, artist, and king. Jesus said (from Matthew's gospel), "Consider the lilies of the field, how they grow; they toil not, neither do they spin . . ." (Px 129 at page 363)

The "public school edition" texts written by creationists simply omit Biblical references but the content and message remain the same. For example, *Evolution—The Fossils Say No!* (32) contains the following:

Creation. By creation we mean the bringing into being by a supernatural Creator of the basic kinds of plants and animals by the process of sudden, or fiat, creation.

We do not know how the Creator created, what processes He used, *for He used processes which are not now operating anywhere in the natural universe.* This is why we refer to creation as Special Creation. We cannot discover by scientific investigation anything about the creative processes used by the Creator. (page 40)

Gish's book also portrays the large majority of evolutionists as "materialistic atheists or agnostics."

Scientific Creationism (Public School Edition) by Morris, is another text reviewed by Ms. Wilson's committee and rejected as unacceptable. The following quotes illustrate the purpose and theme of the text:

Forward
Parents and youth leaders today, and even many scientists and educators, have become concerned about the prevalence and influence of evolution-

ary philosophy in modern curriculum. Not only is this system inimical to orthodox Christianity and Judaism, but also, as many are convinced, to a healthy society and true science as well. (at page iii)

The rationalist of course finds the concept of special creation insufferably naive, even "incredible". Such a judgment, however, is warranted only if one categorically dismisses the existence of an omnipotent God. (at page 17)

Without using creationist literature, Ms. Wilson was unable to locate one genuinely scientific article or work which supported Section 4(a). In order to comply with the mandate of the Board she used such materials as an article from *Readers Digest* about "atomic clocks" which inferentially suggested that the earth was less than 4½ billion years old. She was unable to locate any substantive teaching material for some parts of Section 4 such as the worldwide flood. The curriculum guide which she prepared cannot be taught and has no educational value as science. The defendants did not produce any text or writing in response to this evidence which they claimed was usable in the public school classroom *(33)*.

The conclusion that creation science has no scientific merit or educational value as science has legal significance in light of the Court's previous conclusion that creation science has, as one major effect, the advancement of religion. The second part of the three-pronged test for establishment reaches only those statutes having as their *primary* effect the advancement of religion. Secondary effects which advance religion are not constitutionally fatal. Since creation science is not science, the conclusion is inescapable that the *only* real effect of Act 590 is the advancement of religion. The Act therefore fails both the first and second portions of the test in *Lemon v. Kurtzman*, 403 U.S. 602 (1971).

IV(E)

Act 590 mandates "balanced treatment" for creation science and evolution science. The Act prohibits instruction in any religious doctrine or references to religious writings. The Act is self-contradictory and compliance is impossible unless the public schools elect to forego significant portions of subjects such as biology, world history, geology, zoology, botany, psychology, anthropology, sociology, philosophy, physics and chemistry. Presently, the concepts of evolutionary theory as described in 4(b) permeate the public school textbooks. There is no way teachers can teach the Genesis account of creation in a secular manner.

The State Department of Education, through its textbook selection committee, school boards and school administrators will be required to constantly monitor materials to avoid using religious references. The school boards, administrators and teachers face an impossible task. How is the teacher to respond to questions about a creation suddenly and out of nothing? How will a teacher explain the occurrence of a worldwide flood? How will a teacher explain the concept of a relatively recent age of the earth? The answer is obvious because the only source of this information is ultimately contained in the Book of Genesis.

References to the pervasive nature of religious concepts in creation science texts amply demonstrate why State entanglement with religion is inevitable under Act 590. Involvement of the State in screening texts for impermissible religious references will require State officials to make delicate religious judgments. The need to monitor classroom discussion in order to uphold the Act's prohibition against religious instruction will necessarily involve administrators in questions concerning religion. These continuing involvements of State Officials in questions and issues of religion create an excessive and prohibited entanglement with religion. *Brandon v. Board of Education*, 487 F. Supp 1219, 1230 (N.D.N.Y.), *aff'd.*, 635 F. 2d 971 (2nd Cir. 1980).

V

These conclusions are dispositive of the case and there is no need to reach legal conclusions with respect to the remaining issues. The plaintiffs raised two other issues questioning the constitutionality of the Act and, insofar as the factual findings relevant to these issues are not covered in the preceding discussion, the Court will address these issues. Additionally, the defendants raised two other issues which warrant discussion.

V(A)

First, plaintiff teachers argue the Act is unconstitutionally vague to the extent that they cannot comply with its mandate of "balanced" treatment without jeopardizing their employment. The argument centers around the lack of a precise definition in the Act for the word "balanced." Several witnesses expressed opinions that the word has such meanings as equal time, equal weight, or equal legitimacy. Although the Act could have been more explicit, "balanced" is a word subject to ordinary understanding. The proof is not convincing that a teacher using a reasonably acceptable understanding of the word and making a good faith effort to comply with the Act will be in jeopardy of termination. Other portions of the Act are arguably vague, such as the "relatively recent" inception of the earth and life. The evidence establishes, however, that relatively recent means from 6,000 to 20,000 years, as commonly understood in creation science literature. The meaning of this phrase, like Section 4(a) generally, is, for purposes of the Establishment Clause, all too clear.

V(B)

The plaintiffs' other argument revolves around the alleged infringement by the defendants upon the academic freedom of teachers and students. It is contended this unprecedented intrusion in the curriculum by the State prohibits teachers from teaching what they believe should be taught or requires them to teach that which they do not believe is proper. The evidence reflects that traditionally the State Department of Education, local school boards and administration officials exercise little, if any, influence upon the subject matter taught by classroom teachers. Teachers have been given freedom to teach and emphasize those portions of subjects the individual teacher considered important. The limits to this discretion have generally been derived from the approval of textbooks by the State Department and preparation of curriculum guides by the school districts.

Several witnesses testified that academic freedom for the teacher means, in substance, that the individual teacher should be permitted unlimited discretion subject only to the bounds of professional ethics. The Court is not prepared to adopt such a broad view of academic freedom in the public schools.

In any event, if Act 590 is implemented, many teachers will be required to teach material in support of creation science which they do not consider academically sound. Many teachers will simply forego teaching subjects which might trigger the "balanced treatment" aspects of Act 590 even though they think the subjects are important to a proper presentation of a course.

Implementation of Act 590 will have serious and untoward consequences for students, particularly those planning to attend college. Evolution is the cornerstone of modern biology, and many courses in public schools contain subject matter relating to such varied topics as the age of the earth, geology and relationships among living things. Any student who is deprived of instruction as to the prevailing scientific thought on these topics will be denied a significant part of science education. Such a deprivation through the high school level would undoubtedly have an impact upon the quality of education in the State's colleges and universities, especially including the pre-professional and professional programs in the health sciences.

V(C)

The defendants argue in their brief that evolution is, in effect, a religion, and that by teaching a religion which is contrary to some students' religious views, the State is infringing upon the student's free exercise rights under the First Amendment. Mr. Ellwanger's legislative findings, which were adopted as a finding of fact by the Arkansas Legislature in Act 590, provides:

Evolution-science is contrary to the religious convictions or moral values or philosophical beliefs of many students and parents, including individuals of many different religious faiths and with diverse moral and philosophical beliefs. Act 590, §7(d).

The defendants argue that the teaching of evolution alone presents both a free exercise problem and an establishment problem which can only be redressed by giving balanced treatment to creation science, which is admittedly consistent with some religious beliefs. This argument appears to have its genesis in a student note written by Mr. Wendell Bird, "Freedom of Religion and Science Instruction in Public Schools," 87 Yale L.J. 515 (1978). The argument has no legal merit.

If creation science is, in fact, science and not religion, as the defendants claim, it is difficult to see how the teaching of such a science could "neutralize" the religious nature of evolution.

Assuming for the purposes of argument, however, that evolution is a religion or religious tenet, the remedy is to stop the teaching of evolution, not establish another religion in opposition to it. Yet it is clearly established in the case law, and perhaps also in common sense, that evolution is not a religion and that teaching evolution does not violate the Establishment Clause, *Epperson v. Arkansas, supra, Willoughby v. Stever,* No. 15574-75 (D.D.C. May 18, 1973; *aff'd.* 504 F. 2d 271 (D.C. Cir. 1974), *cert. denied,* 420 U.S. 924 (1975); *Wright v. Houston Indep. School Dist.,* 366 F. Supp. 1208 (S.D. Tex. 1978), *aff'd.* 486 F. 2d 137 (5th Cir. 1973), *cert. denied* 417 U.S. 969 (1974).

V(D)

The defendants presented Dr. Larry Parker, a specialist in devising curricula for public schools. He testified that the public school's curriculum should reflect the subjects the public wants taught in schools. The witness said that polls indicated a significant majority of the American public thought creation science should be taught if evolution was taught. The point of this testimony was never placed in a legal context. No doubt a sizeable majority of Americans believe in the concept of a Creator or, at least, are not opposed to the concept and see nothing wrong with teaching school children about the idea.

The application and content of First Amendment principles are not determined by public opinion polls or by a majority vote. Whether the proponents of Act 590 constitute the majority or the minority is quite irrelevant under a constitutional system of government. No group, no matter how large or small, may use the organs of government, of which the public schools are the most conspicuous and influential, to foist its religious beliefs on others.

The Court closes this opinion with a thought expressed eloquently by the great Justice Frankfurter:

We renew our conviction that "we have staked the very existence of our country on the faith that complete separation between the state and religion is best for the state and best for religion." *Everson v. Board of Education*, 330 U.S. at 59. If nowhere else, in the relation between Church and State, "good fences make good neighbors." *[McCollum v. Board of Education*, 333 U.S. 203, 232 (1948)]

An injunction will be entered permanently prohibiting enforcement of Act 590.

It is ordered this January 5, 1982.

—WILLIAM R. OVERTON *in the U.S. District Court, Eastern District of Arkansas, Western Division*

Notes

1. The complaint is based on 42 U.S.C. §1983, which provides a remedy against any person who, acting under color of state law, deprives another of any right, privilege or immunity guaranteed by the United States Constitution or federal law. This Court's jurisdiction arises under 28 U.S.C. §§1331, 1343(3) and 1343(4). The power to issue declaratory judgments is expressed in 28 U.S.C. §§2201 and 2202.

2. The facts necessary to establish the plaintiffs' standing to sue are contained in the joint stipulation of facts, which is hereby adopted and incorporated herein by reference. There is no doubt that the case is ripe for adjudication.

3. The State of Arkansas was dismissed as a defendant because of its immunity from suit under the Eleventh Amendment. *Hans v. Louisiana*, 134 U.S. 1 (1890).

4. The authorities differ as to generalizations which may be made about Fundamentalism. For example, Dr. Geisler testified to the widely held view that there are five beliefs characteristic of all Fundamentalist movements, in addition, of course, to the inerrancy of Scripture: (1) belief in the virgin birth of Christ, (2) belief in the diety of Christ, (3) belief in the substitutional atonement of Christ, (4) belief in the second coming of Christ, and (5) belief in the physical resurrection of all departed souls. Dr. Marsden, however, testified that this generalization, which has been common in religious scholarship, is now thought to be historical error. There is no doubt, however, that all Fundamentalists take the Scriptures as inerrant and probably most take them as literally true.

5. Initiated Act 1 of 1929, Ark. Stat. Ann. §80-1627 *et seq.*, which prohibited the teaching of evolution in Arkansas schools, is discussed *infra* at text accompanying note 26.

6. Subsequent references to the testimony will be made by the last name of the witness only. References to documentary exhibits will be by the name of the author and the exhibit number.

7. Applicants for membership in the CRS must subscribe to the following statement of belief: "(l) The Bible is the written Word of God, and because we believe it to be inspired thruout (sic), all of its assertions are historically and scientifically true in all of the original autographs. To the student of nature, this means that the account of origins in Genesis is a factual presentation of simple historical truths. (2) All basic types of living things, including man, were made by direct creative acts of God during Creation Week as described in Genesis. Whatever biological changes have occurred since Creation have accomplished only changes within the original created kinds. (3) The great Flood described in Genesis, commonly referred to as the Noachian Deluge, was an historical event, worldwide in its extent and effect. (4) Finally, we are an organization of Christian men of science, who accept Jesus Christ as our Lord and Savior. The account of the special creation of Adam and Eve as one man and one woman, and their subsequent Fall into sin, is the basis for our belief in the necessity of a Savior for all mankind. Therefore, salvation can come only thru (sic) accepting Jesus Christ as our Savior." (Px 115)

8. Because of the voluminous nature of the documentary exhibits, the parties were directed by pre-trial order to submit their proposed exhibits for the Courts' convenience prior to trial. The numbers assigned to the pre-trial submissions do not correspond with those assigned to the same documents at trial and, in some instances, the pre-trial submissions are more complete.

9. Px 130, Morris, *Introducing Scientific Creationism Into the Public Schools* (1975), and Bird, "Resolution for Balanced Presentation of Evolution and Scientific Creationism," *ICR Impact Series* No. 71, App. 14 to Plaintiffs' Pretrial Brief.

10. The creationists often show candor in their proselytization. Henry Morris has stated, "Even if a favorable statute or court decision is obtained, it will probably be declared unconstitutional, especially if the legislation or injunction refers to the Bible account of creation." In the same vein he notes, "The only effective way to get creationism taught properly is to have it taught by teachers who are both willing and able to do it. Since most teachers now are neither willing nor able, they must first be both persuaded and instructed themselves." Px 130, Morris, *Introducing Scientific Creationism Into the Public Schools* (1975) (unpaged).

11. Mr. Bird sought to participate in this litigation by representing a number of individuals who wanted to intervene as defendants. The application for intervention was denied by this Court. *McLean v. Arkansas*, ——F. Supp.——, (E.D. Ark. 1981), aff'd. *per curiam*, Slip Op. No. 81-2023 (8th Cir. Oct. 16, 1981).

12. The model act had been revised to insert "creation science" in lieu of creationism because Ellwanger had the impression people thought creationism was too religious a term (Ellwanger Depo. at 79.)

13. The original model act had been introduced in the South Carolina Legislature, but had died without action after the South Carolina Attorney General had opined that the act was unconstitutional.

14. Specifically, Senator Holsted testified that he holds to a literal interpretation of the Bible; that the bill was compatible with his religious beliefs; that the bill does favor the position of literalists; that his religious convictions were a factor in his sponsorship of the bill; and that he stated publicly to the *Arkansas Gazette* (although not on the floor of the Senate) contemporaneously with the legislative debate that the bill does presuppose the existence of a devine creator. There is no doubt that Senator Holsted knew he was sponsoring the teaching of a religious doctrine. His view was that the bill did not violate the First Amendment because, as he saw it, it did not favor one demonination over another.

15. This statute is, of course, clearly unconstitutional under the Supreme Court's decision in *Abbington School Dist. v. Schempp*, 374 U.S. 203 (1963).

16. The joint stipulation of facts establishes that the following areas are the only *information* specifically required by statute to be taught in all Arkansas Schools: (1) the effects of alcohol and narcotics on the human body, (2) conservation of national resources, (3) Bird Week, (4) Fire Prevention, and (5) Flag etiquette. Additionally, certain specific courses, such as American history and Arkansas history, must be completed by each student before graduation from high school.

17. Paul Ellwanger stated in his deposition that he did not know why Section 4(a)(2)(insufficiency of mutation and natural selection) was included as an evidence supporting creation science. He indicated that he was not a scientist, "but these are the postulates that have been laid down by creation scientists," Ellwanger Dept. at 136.

18. Although defendants must make some effort to cast the concept of creation in non-religious terms, this effort surely causes discomfort to some of the Act's more theologically sophisticated supporters. The concept of a creator God distinct from the God of love and mercy is closely similar to the Marcion and Gnostic heresies, among the deadliest to threaten the early Christian church. These heresies had much to do with development and adoption of the Apostle's Creed as the official creedal statement of the Roman Catholic Church in the West. (Gilkey.)

19. The parallels between Section 4(a) and Genesis are quite specific: (1)"sudden creation from nothing" is taken from Genesis, 1:1-10 (Vawter, Gilkey); (2) destruction of the world by a flood of devine origin is a notion peculiar to Judeo-Christian tradition and is based on Chapters 7 and 8 of Genesis (Vawter); (3) the terms "kinds" has no fixed scientific meaning, but appears repeatedly in Genesis (all scientific witnesses); (4)"relatively recent inception" means an age of the earth from 6,000 to 10,000 years and is based on the genealogy of the Old Testament using the rather astronomical ages assigned to the patriarchs (Gilkey and several of defendants' scientific witnesses); (5) Separate ancestry of man and ape focuses on the portion of the theory of evolution which Fundamentalists find most offensive, *Epperson v. Arkansas*, 393 U.S. 97 (1968).

20. "[C]oncepts concerning . . .a supreme being of some sort are manifestly religious . . .These concepts do not shed that religiosity merely

because they are presented as philosophy or as a science . . ."*Malnak v. Yogi*, 440 F. Supp. 1284, 1322 (D.N.J. 1977); *aff'd per curiam*, 592 F. 2d 197 (3d Cir. 1979).

21. See, e.g., Px 76, Morris, *et al.*, *Scientific Creationism*, 203 (1980) ("If creation really is a fact, this means there is a *Creator*, and the universe is His creation.")Numerous other examples of such admissions can be found in the many exhibits which represent creationist literature, but no useful purpose would be served here by a potentially endless listing.

22. Morris, the Director of ICR and one who first advocated the two model approach, insists that a true Christian cannot compromise with the theory of evolution and that the Genesis version of creation and the theory of evolution are mutually exclusive. Px 31, Morris, *Studies in the Bible & Science*, 102–103. The two model approach was the subject of Dr. Richard Bliss's doctoral dissertation. (Dx 35). It is presented in Bliss, *Origins: Two Models-Evolution, Creation* (1978). Moreover, the two model approach merely casts in educationalist language the dualism which appears in all creationist literature—creation (i.e. God) and evolution are presented as two alternative and mutually exclusive theories. See, e.g., Px 75, Morris *Scientific Creationsim* (1974) (public school edition); Px 59, Fox, *Fossils: Hard Facts from the Earth*. Particularly illustrative is Px 61, Boardman, *et al.*, *Worlds Without End* (1971) a CSRC publication: "One group of scientists, known as creationists, believe that God, in a miraculous manner, created all matter and energy . . .

"Scientists who insist that the universe just grew, by accident, from a mass of hot gases without the direction or help of a Creator are known as evolutionists."

23. The idea that belief in a creator and acceptance of the scientific theory of evolution are mutually exclusive is a false premise and offensive to the religious views of many. (Hicks) Dr. Francisco Ayala, a geneticist of considerable reknown and a former Catholic priest who has the equivalent of a Ph.D. in theology, pointed out that many working scientists who subscribed to the theory of evolution are devoutly religious.

24. This is so despite the fact that some of the defense witnesses do not subscribe to the young earth or flood hypotheses. Dr. Geisler stated his belief that the earth is several billion years old. Dr. Wickramasinghe stated that no rational scientist would believe the earth is less than one million years old or that all the world's geology could be explained by a worldwide flood.

25. "We do not know how God created, what processes He used, for *God used processes which are not now operating anywhere in the natural universe.* This is why we refer to devine creation as Special Creation. We cannot discover by scientific investigation anything about the creative processes used by God." Px 78, Gish, *Evolution? The Fossils say No!*, 42 (3d ed. 1979) (emphasis in original).

26. The evolutionary notion that man and some modern apes have a common ancestor somewhere in the distant past has consistently been distorted by anti-evolutionists to say that man descended from modern

monkeys. As such, this idea has long been most offensive to Fundamentalists. See, *Epperson v. Arkansas*, 393 U.S. 97 (1968).

27. Not only was this point acknowledged by virtually all the defense witnesses, it is patent in the creationist literature. See, e.g., Px 89, Kofahl & Segraves, *The Creation Explanation*, 40: "The Flood of Noah brought about vast changes in the earth's surface, including vulcanism, mountain building, and the deposition of the major part of sedimentary strata. This principle is called 'Biblical catastrophism.' "

28. See n. 7, *supra*, for the full text of the CRS creed.

29. The theory is detailed in Wickramasinghe's book with Sir Fred Hoyle, *Evolution from Space* (1981), which is Dx 79.

30. Ms. Wilson stated that some professors she spoke with sympathized with her plight and tried to help her find scientific materials to support Section 4(a). Others simply asked her to leave.

31. Px 129, published by Zonderman Publishing House (1974), states that it was "prepared by the Textbook Committee of the Creation Research Society." It has a disclaimer pasted inside the front cover stating that it is not suitable for use in public schools.

32. Px 77, by Duane Gish.

33. The passage of Act 590 apparently caught a number of its supporters off guard as much as it did the school district. The Act's author, Paul Ellwanger, stated in a letter to "Dick," (apparently Dr. Richard Bliss at ICR): "And finally, if you know of any textbooks at any level and for any subjects that you think are acceptable to you and also constitutionally admissible, these are things that would be of *enormous* to these bewildered folks who may be caught, as Arkansas now has been, by the sudden need to implement a whole new ball game with which they are quite unfamiliar." (sic)(Unnumbered attachment to Ellwanger depo.)

APPENDIX B

Science at the Bar: Causes for Concern

Larry Laudan

In the wake of the ACLU's victory in the Arkansas creation law trial, the friends of science are apt to be relishing the outcome. The creationists quite clearly made a botch of their case and there can be little doubt that the Arkansas decision will, at least for a time, blunt legislative pressure to enact similar laws in other states. But once the dust has settled, the trial in general and Judge William Overton's ruling in particular may come back to haunt us; for although the verdict itself is probably to be commended, it was reached for all the wrong reasons and by a chain of argument which is hopelessly suspect. Indeed, Overton's ruling rests on a host of misrepresentations of what science is and how it works.

The heart of Overton's ruling is a formulation of what he calls "the essential characteristics of science." These characteristics serve as touchstones for contrasting evolutionary theory with creationism; they lead Overton ultimately to the claim, specious in its own right, that since creationism is not "science," it must be religion. Overton offers five essential properties that demarcate scientific knowledge from other things: "(1) it is guided by natural

Larry Laudan is Professor of History and Philosophy of Science, University of Pittsburgh. I am very grateful for his kindness in giving me permission to publish his note in the present volume. © 1982 by Larry Laudan.

law; (2) it has to be explanatory by reference to natural law; (3) it is testable against the empirical world; (4) its conclusions are tentative, i.e., are not necessarily the final word; and (5) it is falsifiable." These fall naturally into two families: properties (1) and (2) have to do with lawlikeness and explanatory ability; the other three properties have to do with the fallibility and testability of scientific claims. I shall deal with the second set of issues first, since it is there that the most egregious errors of fact and judgment are to be found.

At various key points in Overton's opinion, he charges creationism with being untestable, dogmatic (and thus non-tentative) and unfalsifiable. All three charges are of dubious merit. Consider, for instance, the interlinked claims that creationism is neither falsifiable nor testable. To say as much is to assert that creationism makes no empirical assertions about empirical matters of fact. Thus, as Overton himself grants (apparently without seeing its implications), the creationists say that the earth is of very recent origin (say 6,000 to 20,000 years old); they argue that most of the geological features of the earth's surface are diluvial in character (i.e., products of the postulated world-wide Noachian deluge); they are committed to a large number of factual historical claims with which the Old Testament is replete; they assert the limited variability of species. They are committed to the view that, since animals and man were created at the same time, the human fossil record must be paleontologically co-extensive with the record of lower animals. It can be fairly said that no one has shown how to reconcile such claims with the available evidence; evidence which speaks persuasively to a long earth history, etc.

In short, these claims are testable, they have been tested, and they failed those tests. Unfortunately, the logic of Overton's analysis precludes us from saying any of the above. By arguing that the tenets of creationism are neither testable nor falsifiable, Overton (like those scientists who similarly charge creationism with being untestable) thus deprives science of its strongest argument against creationism. Indeed, if any doctrine in the history of science has ever been falsified, it is that set of claims associated with "creation science." By asserting that creationism makes no empirical claims, one directly if inadvertently plays into the hands of the creationists by immunizing their ideology from empirical confrontation. The right way to combat creationism is by confuting the empirical claims it does make, not by pretending that it makes no such claims at all.

It is true, of course, that some tenets of creationism are not testable in isolation (e.g., the claim that man emerged by a direct supernatural act of creation). But that scarcely makes creationism "unscientific," since it is now widely acknowledged that many scientific claims are not testable in isolation either, but only when they are embedded in part of a larger system of statements, some of whose consequences can be submitted to test.

Overton's third worry about creationism in the group now under discussion centers on the issue of revisability. Over and over again, he finds creationism and its advocates "unscientific" because they have "refused to change it regardless of the evidence developed during the course of the[ir] investigation." In point of fact, the charge is mistaken. If we look at the claims of modern-day creationists and compare them with those of their 19th-century counterparts, one can see significant shifts in orientation and assertion. One of the most visible opponents of creationism, Stephen Gould, concedes that creationists have modified their views about the amount of variability at the level of species change. Creationists do, in short, change their minds from time to time. Doubtless they would credit these shifts to efforts on their part to adjust their views to newly emerging evidence, in what they imagine to be a scientifically respectable way.

Perhaps what Overton had in mind here was the fact that some of the core assumptions of creationism (e.g., that there was a Noachian flood, that man did not evolve from lower animals, that God created the world) seemed closed off from any serious modification. But historical and sociological researches on science strongly suggest that the scientists of any epoch likewise regard some of their beliefs as so fundamental as not to be open to repudiation or negotiation. Would Newton, for instance, have been tentative about the claim that there were forces in the world? Are quantum mechanicians willing to contemplate giving up the uncertainty relation? Are physicists willing to specify circumstances under which they would give up energy conservation? Numerous historians and philosophers of science (Kuhn, Mitroff, Feyerabend, Lakotos) have documented the existence of a certain degree of dogmatism about core commitments in scientific research and have argued that such dogmatism plays a constructive role in promoting the aims of science. I am not denying that there may be subtle but important differences between the dogmatism of scientists and that exhibited by many creationists; but one does not even begin to get at those differences by pretending that science is characterized by an upcompromising open mindedness.

Even worse, the charge of dogmatism against creationism egregiously confuses doctrines with the proponents of those doctrines. Since no law mandates that creationists should be invited into the classroom, it is quite irrelevant whether they themselves are close-minded. What is proposed in the Arkansas statute is that creationism be taught, not that creationists should teach it. So what counts is whether the theses of creationism can be tested, not whether creationists change their minds in light of new evidence. Because, as I have said, many of the theses of creationism are testable, the mind set of creationists has no bearing in law or in fact on the merits of creationism.

What about the other pair of essential characteristics which Overton cites, namely that science is a matter of natural law and explanation by natural law? His precise views are difficult to get at because his formulation of these points is rather fuzzy. But the general idea seems to be this: it is inappropriate and unscientific to postulate the existence of any process or fact which cannot be explained in terms of some known scientific laws. For instance, Overton says that the creationists' assertion that there are outer limits to the change of species "cannot be explained by natural law." He says, a bit earlier, "there is no scientific explanation for these limits which is guided by natural law," and thus such limits are unscientific. Still later, remarking on the hypothesis of the Noachian flood, he says: "A worldwide flood as an explanation of the world's geology is not the product of natural law, nor can its occurrence be explained by natural law." Quite how Overton knows that a worldwide flood "cannot" be explained by the laws of science is left opaque; but even if he were right that we do not know how to reduce a universal flood to the familiar laws of physics, this requirement is an altogether inappropriate standard to bring to bear in ascertaining whether a claim is scientific. For centuries, scientists have realized that there is a difference between establishing the existence of a phenomenon and explaining that phenomenon in a lawlike way. Our ultimate goal, doubtless, is to do both. But to suggest, as Overton does repeatedly, that an existence claim (e.g., there was a worldwide flood) is unscientific until we have found the laws on which the alleged phenomenon depends is simply outrageous. Galileo and Newton took themselves to have established the existence of a gravitational force long before anyone was able to give a causal or explanatory account of gravitation. Darwin took himself to have established the existence of natural selection almost half a century before geneticists were able to lay out the laws of heredity on which natural selection depended. If we took Overton's criterion seriously, we should have to say that Newton and Darwin were unscientific; and, to take an example from our own time, it follows that plate tectonics is unscientific because we have not yet managed to identify the laws of physics and chemistry which account for the dynamics of crustal motion.

The real objection to such creationist claims as that of the (relative) invariability of species is not that such invariability has not been explained by scientific laws, but rather that the evidence for invariability is less robust than the evidence for its contrary, variability. But to say as much requires one to renounce Overton's other charge—to wit, that creationism is not testable.

One could go on at much greater length with this tale of woeful fallacies in Overton's ruling; but that is hardly necessary. What is worrisome is that Overton's line—which neatly coincides with the predominant tactic among scientists who have entered the public fray on this issue—leaves indefinitely many loopholes for the creationists to exploit. As numerous authors have shown, the requirements of testability, revisability, and falsifiabiity are exceedingly weak requirements. Leaving aside the fact that (as I pointed out above) creationism arguably already satisfies these requirements, it would be easy enough for a creationist to say the following: "I will abandon my views if we find a living specimen of a species intermediate between man and the apes." It is, of course, extremely unlikely that we will discover such an individual. But the formal requirements of testability, falsifiability and revisability would all be satisfied in one fell swoop by this move by the creationist. The point is that if we set very weak standards for scientific status—and let there be no mistake about it, all of Overton's last three criteria fall in this category—then it will be quite simple for creationism to qualify as "scientific."

Rather than taking on the creationists obliquely and in wholesale fashion by suggesting that what they are doing is "unscientific" *tout court* (which is doubly silly since few authors can even agree on what makes an activity scientific), we should confront their claims directly and in piecemeal fashion by asking what kind of evidence and arguments can be marshalled for and against each of them. The core issue is not whether creationism satisfies some undemanding and highly controversial definitions of what is scientific; the real question is whether the existing evidence provides stronger arguments for evolutionary theory than for creationism. Once that question is settled, we will know what belongs in the classroom and what does not. Debating the scientific status of creationism (especially when "science" is construed in such an unfortunate manner) is a red herring which diverts attention away from the real issues which should concern us.

The victory in Little Rock was a hollow one, for it was achieved only at the expense of perpetuating and canonizing a false stereotype of what science is and how it works. If it goes unchallenged by the scientific community, it will raise grave doubts about that community's intellectual integrity; for no one familiar with the issues can really believe that anything important got settled through Overton's anachronistic efforts to revive a variety of discredited criteria for distinguishing between the scientific and the non-scientific. Fifty years ago, Clarence Darrow asked apropos the Scopes trial, "Isn't it difficult to realize that a trial of this kind is possible in the 20th century in the United States of America?" We can raise that question anew, but with the added irony that the pro-science forces this time around are defending a philosophy of science which is, in its way, every bit as outmoded as the "science" of the creationists.

Index